DR. ROBERT
ATKINS

DR. ROBERT ATKINS

THE TRUE STORY OF THE MAN BEHIND THE WAR ON CARBOHYDRATES

LISA ROGAK

Chamberlain Bros.
a member of
Penguin Group (USA) Inc.

CHAMBERLAIN BROS.
Published by the Penguin Group
Penguin Group (USA) Inc., 375 Hudson Street, New York, New York 10014, USA
Penguin Group (Canada), 10 Alcorn Avenue, Toronto, Ontario M4V 3B2, (a division of
Pearson Penguin Canada Inc.)
Penguin Books Ltd, 80 Strand, London WC2R 0RL, England
Penguin Group Ireland, 25 St Stephen's Green, Dublin 2, Ireland (a division of
Penguin Books Ltd)
Penguin Group (Australia), 250 Camberwell Road, Camberwell, Victoria 3124, Australia
(a division of Pearson Australia Group Pty Ltd)
Penguin Books India Pvt Ltd, 11 Community Centre, Panchsheel Park,
New Delhi–110 017, India
Penguin Group (NZ), Cnr. Airborne and Rosedale Roads, Albany, Auckland 1310,
New Zealand (a division of Pearson New Zealand Ltd)
Penguin Books (South Africa) (Pty) Ltd, 24 Sturdee Avenue, Rosebank, Johannesburg
2196, South Africa
Penguin Books Limited, Registered Offices: 80 Strand, London WC2R 0RL, England

An application has been submitted to register this book with the Library of Congress.

ISBN 1-59609-038-3

Printed in the United States of America
10 9 8 7 6 5 4 3 2 1

Book design by Melissa Gerber

For Dorothy Lapine, my biggest cheerleader

CONTENTS

Introduction 1

Prologue 5

1. Hail to the Low-Carb King 9

2. The Thirty-Pound Breakthrough 34

3. Happiness Is a Purple Stick 56

4. The Brickbats Fly 77

5. The Twilight Zone 111

6. A Pact with the Devil .136

7. The Sweet Spot 158

8. The Planets Align: July 7, 2002 183

9. The Last Days 193

10. The Battle for the Low-Carb Crown 200

Notes 217

Timeline of Dr. Atkins's Life 223

Dr. Atkins's Published Titles 225

Bibliography 227

Acknowledgments 229

Introduction

The best way to describe Dr. Robert Atkins is that he was a pit bull of a man. He chanced upon his controversial ideas about carbohydrates and diet in the early 1960s and hung on, unyielding to critics, until the day he died, forty years later. Though he lived long enough to see his ideas become accepted, it's not surprising that he continues to be controversial long after his death.

In the winter of 2004, more than eight months after his death, news stories hit with lightning speed whenever the tiniest bit of news came out about the doctor. In January, New York Mayor Michael Bloomberg was accidentally caught on tape referring to the official explanation of the doctor's death in April 2003 as a whitewash—"The guy was fat!" he said—and the widow, Veronica Atkins, hit the talk show circuit to announce her outrage. The next month, a little-known health organization called "Physicians for Responsible Medicine" released an illegally obtained copy of Atkins's death records. Mrs. Atkins again made the media rounds to denounce the group and their actions.

In the middle of all the controversy and finger-pointing, one thing stood out: While everyone had something to say—good or bad—about the diet, little was actually said about Atkins himself, who he was and what he was like.

Out of idle curiosity, I began to do some digging so see if I could find out something about the man. I spoke with people who knew him and had worked side by side with him for years, and I read through articles and transcripts from his early days of notoriety, in 1972, when his first book, *Dr. Atkins' Diet Revolution,* was published.

As is the case today, I had to dig through an awful lot of negativity hurled at Atkins through the years to get to a few neutral nuggets about his life, but, eventually, a picture of a complicated man began to emerge: He was both outspoken and shy, generous and defensive, and, above all, he loved working with his patients.

As I dug, the life of the man turned from the sound bite the world knew him by to someone who was totally honest with himself and with others, and who miraculously never once altered his course since the day he discovered what to him was the absolute truth about weight loss.

I ended up learning a lot from him. For example, I thought that I was stubborn, but Atkins was so obstinate and unyielding that he had me beat a thousand times over. While researching this book, there were many days when I looked at the teetering stacks of interviews, articles, transcripts, and assorted notes on my desk that threatened to topple over at the slightest breeze and audibly groaned at the thought of starting to make sense of it all.

But then I thought of Atkins, who slogged it out for years—decades, even—and he continued on with it while faced with a constant barrage of attacks and criticism and ostracism from every possible front.

Suddenly, my task seemed minuscule in comparison.

Prologue

For Dr. Robert Atkins, the morning of April 8, 2003, had started out like any other.

Even though he was seventy-two years old and could have retired on his wealth many years ago, Dr. Atkins got up early that morning—as he did four days each week—to put in a full day of seeing patients at the Atkins Center. In between appointments with patients, he would read medical journals, talk to his staff, and call colleagues and longtime associates on the phone to chat.

Atkins was also working on what he considered to be his most important book to date, a massive volume on diabetes. After all, as he had steadfastly maintained through the decades of his controversial medical practice and highly public profile, the condition could actually be avoided and even reversed by following a diet that was high in fat and protein and very low in carbohydrates. He had seen countless patients reverse their diabetes by adopting such a diet and, in turn, totally eliminate other chronic ailments that had plagued them for years.

Since several positive studies on low-carb diets had recently been published in the very medical journals that had lambasted him and his theories through the years, Atkins felt comfortable in proceeding to this next stage of his lifelong fight.

His critics were still as vociferous as ever, but they were increasingly being drowned out by the plethora of positive press from the media and medicine.

His wife of fifteen years, Veronica, had wanted him to retire for a long time, or at least cut down his workload to only a day or two each week. Fortunately for her, it looked like her workaholic husband was about to follow her advice.

Atkins had just returned from spending the weekend in Florida. He thought about staying for a few more days, but he needed to get back to his patients, for the week was already booked up, as usual.

Dr. Atkins looked tired. Numerous friends and colleagues had recently commented on his drained appearance, which he had always shrugged off by attributing it to the battle he had fought through the years to get his unconventional ideas recognized. Now, however, it seemed that the fight was winding down and it looked like other, very powerful institutions and people were gathering in his corner, which would put him in an entirely new position. While he would continue to be on the defensive, at least he wouldn't have to fight alone anymore.

So it looked like a good time to cut back his workload and spend more time relaxing and traveling with Veronica. Though they purchased a new condominium in Palm Beach the previous fall, he had not yet spent a night there.

As he walked out the lobby of his Sutton Place apartment that morning, he looked with dismay at the almost foot of snow that had piled up in the gutter, already speckled with soot. Maybe he should have stayed in Florida a few more days, he thought, as he headed out onto the street. He pulled his overcoat tightly around him.

By the time he reached the Atkins Center—a fifteen-minute walk on that unseasonably wintry April day—his life would hang by a thread.

Robert Coleman Atkins, M.D., was an intriguing, stubborn, shy, and complex man who didn't like to reveal much about himself, lest the focus turn away from the topic he considered to be all-important: a diet low in carbohydrates that would not only help make it easier to lose weight but would also radically improve a person's health.

As a result, because of the dearth of information about his life, he was greatly misunderstood by the American public and medical professionals. Even most of the colleagues who worked side by side with him for years knew very little about what made the man tick, aside from his unwavering position on his favored diet. Most would be surprised by the fact that Atkins grew up as a child of the Depression and a descendant of Russian Jewish immigrants and that these influences forged his identity just as strongly as did his need to tell the world about the benefits of a low-carb diet.

Celebrities throughout three decades followed his diet, from Buddy Hackett and Kaye Ballard in the 1960s and '70s to Suzanne Somers, Sarah Jessica Parker, and Renée Zellweger at the beginning of the twenty-first century. Some even appointed him to be their personal physician and visited the Atkins Center regularly.

His humor could be self-deprecating at times, and when he addressed his detractors he liked to inject a bit of humor. In his second book, *Super Energy*, published in 1977, he wrote, "[Do] they think I'm getting rich? I would have made more per hour collecting old Captain Marvel comic books."

But Robert Atkins was also so committed to the idea that his diet would save the world—or at least improve the health and waistlines of overweight Americans—that he would frequently approach complete strangers just to criticize what they put in their mouths.

One day, he spied a little boy eating from a box of malted milk balls, so he marches right up to the kid to tell him that the sugar in his candy is harmful.

"What's wrong with sugar?" the boy asked.

"Nothing, as long as you don't swallow it," Atkins replied.

Robert Atkins essentially bet his whole life on a hypothesis, which he had largely formulated on the basis of premature data. But once he was convinced of the value of that theory, he had a very strong motivation to persuade the rest of the world that he was right. And that's how he spent his entire life.

Over the more than four decades that Atkins was actively seeing patients, he estimated that he saw more than sixty-five thousand men and women. When most people encountered him, they didn't want to know about him, they wanted to know about the diet, and what it could do for them. This was positively fine with Atkins, because he wasn't too keen on people knowing too much about him, anyway. His life was his diet, and spreading the word about it. His story would definitely distract folks from his message.

Or so he thought.

1.

HAIL TO THE LOW-CARB KING

In order to best understand the life of Robert Atkins, M.D., all you need to know is one thing: He was deathly afraid of being hungry.

He was thirty-three years old the first time he decided to do something about the forty excess pounds that he carried, and, like most in his situation, he tried some of the diets that were popular in the early 1960s. However, also like most others, he found that he was constantly hungry when following them. "It's beyond my comprehension how anyone can put up with the kind of hunger I put up with," Atkins told a newspaper in 1973.

"He couldn't stand being hungry. That was his greatest fear, to be hungry," his wife Veronica would confirm many years later.

But it wasn't just physical hunger that consumed Atkins. He was also hungry for other things in life: a successful career, material possessions, women. The overriding theme of his life would be that no matter how much he had, it would never be enough.

Once he was able to control his physical hunger by stumbling on the idea of following a diet low in carbohydrates, his other appetites quickly took center stage as a cruel form of compensation.

In the 1980s, during the peak years of his practice, Atkins was seeing sixty patients a day. Throughout the span of his career—in between the criticism and the diet books that sold millions of copies—he maintained a full-time medical practice, and, whenever possible, he always made a point of telling people the exact number of patients who had passed through that practice.

In time, he would be able to find salves for his other hungers, to some extent, but no matter how many patients he saw, women he dated, or hours he worked he would never feel satisfied.

But that was no surprise, since achievement was a belief system that was deeply rooted in his family, going back at least several generations.

Robert Coleman Atkins was born on October 17, 1930, to Eugene and Norma Atkins. Eugene was a confectioner and peddler, while Norma was a housewife who worked in a variety of secretarial and sales positions whenever money got tight, as it often did during the Great Depression. Both Eugene and Norma had Russian Jewish grandparents who had emigrated to the United States in the 1890s.

Norma and Eugene grew up hearing about the struggles and sacrifices their grandparents had made to escape poverty and persecution in the Old World in order to come to the New. The custom was that whenever a child would act up, more often than not they'd be brought in line with a particularly horrendous tale of the trials and tribulations that their beloved Nana and Poppy had endured.

As was the case with other immigrant families, each successive generation was expected to do better than the previous one, as if to validate the blood and tears of the ancestors who had given up the bulk of their worldly possessions in order to make the journey to America. Therefore, another lesson for the children to learn was the more you have, the better, because then your chances for holding onto at least one prized possession were good in case someone or something takes it all away.

It was common for most families in the lower-class Jewish neighborhoods where Robert grew up in Columbus, Ohio, and then in Dayton, to have at least four or five kids. Birth control was both rudimentary and unreliable—and frowned upon by rabbis—and firstborn sons were viewed as the jewel of the family, the one child whose sole responsibility was to make the family—and the ancestors—proud. The ultimate dream for a Russian Jewish family was for their firstborn son to become a doctor.

Robert was not only the firstborn son, he was also the only child of Eugene and Norma. After the first child, families with lots of children tend to spread out their ambitions and dreams among the ones that follow. With Robert, he was *it*. He served as the sole conduit for all of his parents' hopes and wishes, and their disappointments, too. There were no other siblings to share the burden of his parents' expectations.

Robert Atkins learned how to carry the weight of the world on his shoulders at a very early age.

In the fall of 1891, a thirty-five-year-old Russian Jew named Coleman Tokerman said good-bye to his family in Elizavetgrad,

Russia, and traveled by steamship to America to establish a new life in Columbus, Ohio. The usual tradition was for a young man to borrow enough money from relatives, friends, rabbis, even town officials, to pay for his trip. Once he arrived in America—most often settling where others from his village or town had landed before him—he would find a job or, more likely, start a business as a peddler. He would save up his money so he could pay back the money he had borrowed for his journey, and then continue to save so that he could buy a ticket to bring his wife over, the girl he was planning to marry, or the fiancée that a matchmaker or his parents had selected for him, since many in eastern Europe relied on arranged marriages.

Coleman Tokerman already had a wife and family, so in June 1892 he sent money and tickets so his wife, Rosa, and two sons could make the journey to the United States and join him in Columbus. Traveling from Hamburg to Philadelphia in steerage, the family crossed the sea in just over a week. Once they were settled in Columbus, one of the first things Coleman did was to change the family's last name to Tuckerman in order to better assimilate in their new country, a common move among immigrants of the time.

Given the events in eastern Europe in the late 1800s, Coleman was determined to migrate, along with more than ten million other people who came to the United States between 1881 and 1914. Some came to America to escape forced military inscription or imprisonment, but the majority emigrated in order to improve their lives and to increase their opportunities for financial success. A series of legislation known as the "May Laws" had been passed throughout eastern Europe in 1882, which dictated that Jews from all over the Russian Empire were required to move from the countryside into cities that included Warsaw, Kiev, and Minsk. This sudden influx of people resulted in severe overcrowding as well as cutthroat competition. The population in Lodz, one of the cities designated for Jews, went from 128,000 in 1882 to 220,000 just fifteen years later. In addition, highly skilled professionals were banned from holding jobs as well as owning land, so that by 1900 one in every five Jews was classified as a pauper by local government.

More onerous, however, were the pogroms ordered by the government which resulted in violence, lootings, arson, and murder as officially sanctioned forms of discrimination against Jews.

So Coleman had good reason for coming to the United States, and his efforts at the time would turn him into a legend among future generations of his family. Many men who followed the same path took an average of three years before they were able to pay off the debt for their trip and then save the money that would bring their families over. Coleman, however, paid off his debt and sent for his family a mere nine months after he landed in Columbus. Curiously, in the 1904–1905 edition of the Columbus city directory, Coleman's occupation was listed as huckster, which was another term for salesman.

For the next several generations, members of the Tuckerman family looked to Coleman the patriarch as an example of what could be accomplished with a lot of determination and very little money, if any.

One of the children Coleman brought over on the seventy-five-dollar steerage ticket was Samuel, who was just eleven when he immigrated to Columbus. The boy quickly learned that while they might be poor, they made do with what they had and they worked as hard as they could to make a better life for their families. Peddlers went up and down the streets all day long selling milk, fruit, and other perishable items from carts they either pushed or that were drawn by horse. When he was still a teenager, Samuel pushed a fruit cart through the neighborhoods of Columbus.

When Samuel Tuckerman was about twenty-three years old, he married Esther Thall, and they set up a household together at 494 Beck Street, in the heart of Columbus's Jewish community that was known as Bexley.

When Norma Tuckerman was born to Samuel and Esther Tuckerman on July 31, 1910, like her older sister, Dorothy, and younger brother, Sanford, and her other relatives as well, she had the reputation of her grandfather Coleman to look up to—and live up to. As a Jewish girl growing up in Columbus, however, her options were quite limited, so it would be hard for her to strive for greatness by herself. For that, she'd have to turn to others.

Eugene Atkins was born on October 21, 1906, in Dayton, Ohio, the second of five children born to Hyman and Rose Atkin. (It is not known when the *s* was added to the name; Atkins was often an Americanized version of Aschkenazy.)

They lived in a modest home at 15 Corwin Street, in a predominantly Jewish neighborhood. Eugene was the second of four sons in a family of five children. Like Norma's parents, Hyman and Rose had emigrated to the United States from Russia in the great wave of migration from eastern Europe, and, as such, both sets of parents shared similar values and points of view.

However, Eugene's family didn't have a familial icon like Coleman to hold up as a shining example of what could be done if you just put your mind to it. Hyman worked as a "tinner"—in other words, he ran a tin shop—and to look around at the other families on the block where fathers worked as peddlers, drugstore clerks, and salesmen, Eugene's parents told their children the best they could do is get through the day and do a little better than your parents.

And so, like many of his peers, Eugene started a business as a peddler. As today's books on the craft of salesmanship show, successful peddlers were cunning and quite smart, but also humble when a situation called for it. And if he could make his customers laugh, the deal was as good as sealed.

It's unclear how Eugene and Norma first met, since he was living in Dayton and she was still at home with her parents in Columbus when they were married on October 7, 1929, by Rabbi Isaac Werne. Rabbi Werne presided over Agudas Achim, the first Orthodox synagogue in Columbus, founded by the initial wave of immigrants from Russia and other parts of eastern Europe. Maybe he was passing through because of his work, or maybe it was a chance meeting or that they had friends in common. But what is clear is that theirs wasn't an arranged marriage because Norma's father, Samuel, didn't want her to marry him.

While she couldn't go out into the world to make her mark the same way as her male relatives, it turned out that Norma was nonetheless chomping at the bit to get out of her father's house to make it on her own. She must have been just as stubborn and determined as her grandfather. Her marriage license lists her birthdate as July 31, 1908, but she was actually only nineteen years old, born on the same day in 1910. In those days, a girl under the age of twenty-one who wanted to get married needed to get permission from her father and, for some reason, she knew that his blessing would not be forthcoming; perhaps her father thought she could do better than the son of a lowly tinner. On the marriage license, Eugene listed his occupation as "confectioner," an interesting fact considering that his only son would spend more than half of his life railing against sugar. Norma's occupation was listed as "at home."

But the rabbi took Norma's side. The Tuckerman family were members of his synagogue, and he was well aware of the exact ages of each of Samuel's children. He married them on October 7, 1929, nonetheless. The newlyweds had just barely started their new life when the stock market crashed days later, on October 24, launching the Great Depression that enveloped the world for the next decade.

Norma may have seen a glimmer of ambition in Eugene, even though he failed to earn her father's respect. He was involved in the food business, and, after all, everybody has to eat. Even though the candies he plied were clearly a luxury people could live without, it soon became clear to her that even as the economy soured and people began to struggle to provide themselves with the barest of necessities, even the most destitute craved a treat now and then. Her son Robert would later take that to heart, for he correctly surmised that if people could indulge in treats they thought were forbidden and still lose weight, he could become very successful indeed.

Robert was born on October 17, 1930, just a year after the Depression took hold. His parents gave him the middle name "Coleman," not only to honor Norma's grandfather but also as a constant reminder of what their child could accomplish if he worked hard.

As soon as Robert was old enough, Eugene began taking Robert along on his rounds to customers, and he even let him "close" a deal or two. Young Robert watched his father in action enough times, so he knew what to do. But for the boy, it wasn't the handshake at the close of a successful deal that sealed his fate, it was the laughter that came from the grown men watching the little boy trying to imitate his father that hooked him.

"Chip off the old block," the men would say, clapping each other on the back. Robert would continue with his routine, sometimes doing an impression of one of the men, or merely being so convincing in his "shtick" that he would end up moving more merchandise than his father. In later years, after becoming a household name, it was not hard to pick up a bit of this early hucksterism when Atkins had to defend his diet in front of the TV cameras.

Norma wasn't crazy about the idea of her little boy spending time with rough men, in neighborhoods far worse than the one where she grew up. But at least Eugene was working long days, and he promised he would move the family to a better neighborhood in Columbus as soon as he could come up with the money. And while Norma still didn't think Eugene was working as hard as he could, how could she say no? At least with a little boy at his side, Eugene couldn't get into any trouble.

Or so Norma thought. Though peddling and sales were still the most common occupations among Jewish men at the time, many were about to add a whole new sideline, regardless of whether wares were sold to households from a cart or sold wholesale at the market.

During that era in Columbus, as well as in any city of a certain size, there were several blocks set aside for a city market. In larger cities such as Boston and New York, there was more than one market—one specialized in meat, another produce—but in Columbus the dozen or so commissioned merchants—half of whom were Jewish, the other half being Italian—plied their wares from crudely built wooden stands inside one hall.

The merchants, who considered themselves rungs above the lowly street peddlers, primarily conducted wholesale business, where buyers at local restaurants, hotels, and grocery stores would make their selections in the morning to be delivered later that day.

The constant traffic meant that it was hard to keep track of a peddler who visited a particular merchant, and vice versa, as peddlers and suppliers and workers came and went from the market all day long. Gambling had long been a popular side business for many Jewish peddlers in both the Old and New Worlds. As door-to-door peddlers of provisions, they had ample opportunity to take bets and pay out winnings. As the years of the Depression wore on and hardship increased, gambling, particularly betting on numbers, grew exponentially throughout the city. Residents came to view a wager as a chance to escape poverty, or maybe just a brief respite from everyday miseries. Local law enforcement tended to turn a blind eye to small-time gambling rackets, so an enterprising peddler/bookie could build quite a lucrative enterprise that more than likely would soon overshadow his primary, legitimate one. And once Prohibition ended in 1933—another sideline that many peddlers dabbled in during those "dry" years—they had to turn to something to supplement their lost income and gambling was it.

"After 1933, bookmaking emerged as the major criminal activity of Columbus Jews," wrote Marc Lee Raphael in his book *Jews and Judaism in a Midwestern Community: Columbus, Ohio, 1840–1975.* Neighbors and rabbis tended to look the other way at those who led these pursuits, and even bookies who were arrested typically were not shuttled into the local penal system but instead handed back to their community for treatment by the local Jewish social service agencies. While it's not clear if this tactic on the part of law enforcement was discriminatory or just a way to keep down the budget of the local jails, soon non-Jews who were caught in a gambling sting would often claim to be Jewish in order to avoid spending time in jail.

Toward the end of the 1930s, with the promise of better financial times ahead, public acceptance of the vice began to wane and the police began to move in and crack down on those responsible, particularly the bookies. By 1938, there were close to fifty thousand arrests each year for gambling, and city politicians promised to eradicate gambling as a blemish on the city in the next round of elections the following year.

It's unknown whether Robert's father was caught in the crackdown and whether that was the primary reason the family relocated to Dayton in 1941. Later on, Atkins would joke with a colleague that Eugene worked as a bookie, which made sense given the name of the first establishment Eugene launched in Dayton, the Four

Aces Bar, at 1115 West 3rd Street, a major thoroughfare where numerous bars were located. In later interviews, however, Atkins was sometimes vague about what his father did for a living. "My father owned a few little restaurants and places where people could stay overnight," he told one reporter just two months before he died.

The family moved into a modest apartment at 1308 North Euclid Avenue, a ten-minute walk from the bar, and Robert enrolled in the seventh grade. He had already skipped a grade in elementary school, and Robert set about establishing himself as a model student, a way to channel the ambition that Norma had fostered in him since she felt she hadn't made much headway with Eugene.

In the beginning, the family was content and pleased in their new home. Dayton View, their new neighborhood, was a step up from the gritty streets of Columbus where Norma had spent her entire life. Two synagogues were already established in the area—Beth Jacob and Temple Israel—but it was Beth Abraham the family eventually joined when it was built in 1943.

Compared to sleepy Columbus, which rolled up its sidewalks once state government closed up shop for the day, Dayton was also a step up in terms of excitement. With a population of 250,000 in 1940, it had long been a company town, run by National Cash Register, but with World War II looming Dayton grew by leaps and bounds because of Wright Patterson Air Force Base, which would serve as the military's center of research for the duration of the war. The city's industrial infrastructure and its central location for major transportation systems drew people from all over the Midwest. General Motors became a major force in the town, with five separate plants in full operation, and Frigidaire and Delco also opened factories that soon required thousands of employees. It was a bustling, fast-growing city that offered many opportunities not available in Columbus.

Once war was officially declared and factories all over the country retooled to produce planes, weapons, and other wartime goods, people flocked to the city either to work in the factories or cater to those who did. And because these newcomers didn't seem to need candy so much as they'd needed a drink, Eugene switched gears and opened a bar.

Curiously, in the entry for the bar appearing in the 1941 Dayton city directory—the first year the family lived in Dayton—Norma is listed as the owner, not Eugene. It also noted that she was still living in Columbus. It's unclear why Eugene's name didn't appear. Perhaps he couldn't legally register as the owner because of a prior conviction for gambling, or perhaps he just stayed behind in Columbus for a while. Whatever the reason, the following year both Norma's and Eugene's names appeared in the directory.

As Eugene built his business, he spent long hours holding court at the bar. It was a real change for him to be based in one place, with his customers coming to him to do business instead of the other way around. And business was so good that the following year he opened a cigar store, Press and Atkins, with partner Lewis Press, right next door, at 1111 West 3rd Street. Norma often complained that Eugene wasn't spending enough time at home with his family, but he reminded her that as soon as he could sock away a little money they could move from the cramped Euclid Avenue apartment to a home of their own, or at least an apartment in a luxury building.

So Norma contented herself with keeping a spotless kosher

home and raising her son, channeling the drive to succeed instilled in her by her grandfather to her son. Despite the low-rent characters her husband preferred to hang out with at the bar and cigar store, she was determined to keep up her appearance by dressing modestly but stylishly, and she encouraged Robert to do the same. She told him that if he always dressed well and looked presentable, people would respect him and take him seriously.

Norma never aired the family's dirty laundry in public. People from good families—or those who aspired to be—never let on that anything was less than perfect. So to compensate, she always made sure her makeup was impeccable and every hair was in place before she left the apartment. More important, she made sure that people could tell at a glance that she had real style, according to Loretta Weber, who dated Robert briefly when he was in college.

"I think his parents fought," says Weber. "In families like that, the women had different aspirations from their husbands, and were often more upwardly mobile." Eugene was an ordinary middle-class guy, and he didn't really try to be anything more than what he was, despite the fact that he owned two thriving businesses. Of course, that didn't satisfy Norma's ambitions. Weber said she'd seen it before in many Jewish families of the era. "The husband may be working really hard to bring home the bread, but his attractive wife wants a lot more." she said, adding that even if they were living in a real dump Norma was the type of woman who always kept a lovely home, who had a service of fine china.

Along with instilling this sense of order, Norma also taught her son to fit into society, that by no means should he call attention to his ethnicity—a common practice at a time when anyone from a religious background other than Protestant was viewed automatically as different, as suspect.

Robert was an obedient child. "If somebody wore a cashmere sweater," he said, "I would wear one. If somebody wore argyle socks, I would wear [them]." While he was an ace student in junior high and high school, no matter how hard he tried he didn't fit in very well. He once described his former classmates as favoring "people who were athletes rather than brains."

Despite these efforts to assimilate into American culture seamlessly, and given the great struggles the family had gone through, it was also important to the Atkinses to honor and respect their Jewish heritage. Beth Abraham, the conservative synagogue they joined within walking distance of their apartment, was not as observant as an Orthodox synagogue would have been, roughly equivalent to Christians who attend on Christmas and Easter only. It's likely that the Atkinses attended synagogue on the high holidays of Rosh Hashanah and Yom Kippur only.

While Norma devoted much time to teaching young Robert that it was vital he make something of himself, she also passed along the lessons of her childhood, including stories her parents told her about her grandfather Coleman. And because she wanted Robert to inherit her sense of style, not Eugene's, she taught him not only about clothes but about art as well.

Even as a young girl, Norma had appreciated fine art. She favored Impressionists, collecting prints and hanging them around the apartment.

One such print depicted opening night at New York's Metropolitan Museum at the turn of the century. Gaslights aglow, women in evening gowns, the scene glamorously portrays what living the good life in New York must have been all about among the Vanderbilts and other wealthy families. Perhaps both mother and son thought that the people depicted had enough to be happy, living in such style! Another print Norma hung was of a seaport in France. Slightly fuzzy in the Impressionist style, it too portrayed the happy, relaxing life that was possible when you had enough of everything. For mother and son, it was the kind of life that seemed far, far away from their small apartment in Dayton, Ohio.

While there were other paintings Norma also favored, most had one thing in common: they showed romantic paradises that were about as far as you could get from the everyday life of the Atkins family. They were refined, with no traces of the crude, undisguised gestures and emotions of patrons of the bar and cigar store. No doubt as Norma taught Robert about art and what the pictures represented, Robert picked up that his mother would have liked to move to some distant land, far away from her husband. And for his part, young Robert undoubtedly couldn't help but be enchanted by the idea of living in such places too, where maybe it didn't matter that he was a brain in a school filled with jocks or even that he was Jewish.

In any case, he and his mother both knew that Dayton wasn't his kind of town, and that he would have to leave as soon as he could. But to do that, he had to accomplish even more than his great-grandfather Coleman Tuckerman had. And that meant he had to get busy.

*   *   *

By the time Robert had reached his senior year at Fairview High School, he had established himself as one of the smartest students in the school.

Each year, the state of Ohio sponsored a general scholarship test where the best students in high schools all over the state could compete in a number of different subjects to determine the smartest student in the entire state. While no one was required to take the test, teachers encouraged certain students they thought had a chance of doing well, hoping that a top-ranking student would bring glory to the school and to the teachers.

A few months before the test, in the spring of 1947, Robert Rafner was singled out for the test along with his classmate Robert Atkins. Since they lived in the same neighborhood, they decided to study together, which they did on a couple of occasions at the Atkins apartment.

"Bob was very ambitious intellectually, much more than I was," says Rafner, who was particularly irked that despite the fact that Atkins spent very little time studying he still was an excellent student. "I was envious, because he played basketball, worked on the school newspaper, went out with any girl who came along, and breezed right through school with top grades, while I had to work so hard at it."

Rafner adds that Atkins stood out among his classmates not just because of his academic achievement but also for the way he carried himself. "He was sure of himself in a way that was not usual for his age," he says. "Bob was so self-confident that it almost bordered on arrogance, but it wasn't due to insecurity, which was the case with most kids." Rafner adds that Atkins's attitude and confidence were also obvious in the way he walked. "He had a jaunty kind of walk because he was so darn sure of himself, and I envied that too because I wasn't that sure of myself."

When the results of the scholarship test came out, Atkins came in second in the state out of 8,500 other seniors from 1,300 high schools who took the test. He was rewarded for his success when his photo was splashed across the pages of the *Dayton Herald* on April 8, 1947. Wearing a sport jacket, he stands proudly with a basketball in his hands.

With this stellar achievement, Bob Atkins was clearly on his way.

For college-bound Jewish boys living in Dayton just before midcentury, options were few: only a handful of colleges—Ohio State or the University of Michigan—were open to them, and there was just one reason for this.

Back in the 1940s, it was a not so well kept secret that there were certain colleges where Jews could not apply. Far outnumbering the schools where they could apply and hope to get into, the most notorious among the don't-even-bother institutions were the Ivy League. It was only after the war, as collective postwar guilt permeated the culture and helped to shift attitudes, that many schools began to relax such restrictions.

Robert Rafner said that Robert Atkins was so smart that he could have easily gotten into Princeton after the war years, which was where Rafner enrolled.

"But the change wasn't always apparent when it came to the Eastern schools," he said, adding that this was especially true of Princeton.

When he applied for the class of 1951, few Jews had ever applied before him because they didn't think they were welcome. "In my class, there were 27 Jews out of 650 students," he noted. The following year, that number increased to fifty-four students. And while big changes were happening academically for Jews, equally big changes were happening socially as well. Yet Atkins would come to see later that, in some cases, anti-Semitism was still alive and well, only it had gone underground.

It's not entirely clear why Robert Atkins didn't apply to an Ivy League school in this more welcoming atmosphere, since the timing for top students like himself couldn't have been better. In addition, counselors at schools with a number of Jewish students, such as Fairview High School, clearly were aware of the trend. But he decided to play it safe instead and apply to the University of Michigan, probably because it was known for its excellent premed program. And from the time he was a young boy, Robert had talked about his dream of being a doctor.

Besides, his mother's words to always try to fit in still resonated: Why make yourself deliberately stand out as one of the elite's token Jews? He would also be closer to home at the University of Michigan—about two hundred miles away—so he could visit his mother on weekends. After all, he was still the only son.

His other dream was to live in New York City.

"The first time I came to New York, I realized I didn't like small towns as much as I like gigantic towns," he said.

And that gigantic town *had* to be New York, or, more specifically, Manhattan. It was as if the first time he visited the city as a teenager, he knew that he would never want to live anywhere else, and he then began to chart the path that would eventually prove to be the most direct to getting there, even if it wasn't the most direct geographically, as in his decision to attend college in Michigan.

The fact that New York was home to a sizable Jewish community must have also been a factor in Atkins's decision to aim his future toward the East Coast. According to Robert Rafner, Jews in 1940s Dayton lived in a mildly anti-Semitic environment, and were reminded of the fact twenty-four hours a day. Though they were few in number—it's estimated that out of a population of a quarter of a million people, only about five thousand were Jewish—they couldn't live in certain neighborhoods, and they couldn't belong to certain country clubs. While most Jews knew that the Dayton View neighborhood was where they would feel most at home, they dared not even dream about living in Oakwood, an upper-income neighborhood on the other side of town where the city's elite Protestant families lived. "We were always conscious that we were Jews by the virtue of where we lived," said Rafner.

A bright Jewish teenage boy like Robert Atkins had two options after college, which he was well aware of when still in high school: he could return to Dayton and start a business or work in his father's business, or he could get the hell out of Dodge and stay out. Robert Rafner met both of Atkins's parents, and while he believes that the ambitions of the younger Atkins came primarily from his mother, the fact that he didn't want to end up like his father—still huckstering in the bar and the cigar store, unofficially banned from pursuing certain occupations or living in certain neighborhoods by sheer virtue of his ethnic heritage—undoubtedly provided an equal boost to his ambition.

The horizons of most of the Jewish boys in Atkins's high school class were pretty limited. According to Rafner, while some did become doctors and lawyers, once they finished their studies and got their professional degrees instead of setting their sights farther afield they returned home to settle down in Dayton. As adults, they attended the same synagogues they attended when they were growing up, and their circle of friends was the same as in high school.

"I was a little bit suffocated by the environment," says Rafner. "And I know that Bob Atkins was, too. We both wanted to get away, and, if anything, this was the primary motivation that drove him to get away and to become something more than just another Jewish kid who went away to college but came back to settle down in Dayton."

After Atkins scored second in the state scholarship test, Rafner saw his classmate change in a not-so-subtle way. "He began to think of himself as big-time," he said. "He started to regard himself as being more important than everybody else, and since he obviously had more potential, he could even think about becoming famous. I think he had this feeling of doing something very important in the world, but I wouldn't have thought that he would wind up doing what he did."

In the fall of 1947, Atkins packed his bags and moved to Ann Arbor to enroll as a member of the class of 1951 at the University of Michigan, majoring in premed. From the first day of classes, he set about distinguishing himself academically just as he had done throughout high school.

But, unlike in high school, Atkins decided that he would also make his mark socially. It helped that once he was there he was surrounded by others who, while they may not have been on the same level intellectually as he was, like him they placed a premium on academic achievement. Slowly but surely, he came out of his shell and began to develop quite an active social life in college. He pledged to Zeta Beta Tau, a fraternity for Jewish students, and moved into the fraternity house.

Once he was on his own and away from home for the first time, Atkins discovered that the humor he used to entertain his father's clients back in Columbus translated into a real gift for comedy, for entertaining other people, especially large groups.

Larry Stein, a real estate developer in Dayton, was Atkins's roommate and pledge brother during their sophomore year. "He was a brilliant guy, and made Phi Beta Kappa," he said, adding that there were two very distinct sides to Atkins, one very private, the other extremely public.

"While he liked to keep to himself most of the time, he also loved to entertain people," Stein said. "We used to have these house parties where Bob would be the major entertainment, and people would come from all over the campus. There were so many people in the house that you couldn't move." Some of the parties fell under the banner of a variety show produced by the fraternity known as *Hillelzapoppin*. Stein said that one of Atkins's favorite acts was to perform an impression of the entertainer Danny Kaye, adding that he could impersonate the celebrity even better than Danny Kaye being himself. Before a party, Atkins would memorize all of Kaye's routines and then repeat them verbatim in front of his classmates, complete with foreign languages and accents. "Bob was the type who could read a book in one evening and take a test the next day and get one hundred percent on it," Stein added. "He had a fabulous memory."

Around the same time, Atkins also began to perfect his impression of Herb Shriner, another top comedian of the 1950s. In fact, Atkins's passion for performing comedy and joking with people was so pitch-perfect that one time when Shriner was hosting a live radio show, Atkins called in while doing his impression and actually got by the phone screener to Shriner's agent, who became very confused, because he thought Atkins actually was the comedian.

After the parties, however, Bob would go back to being the conscientious student. "He would come out of his shell at these parties," said Stein. "Other than that, he mostly kept to himself."

Besides his knack for comedy, Atkins also stood out from the other students because, just as Norma had taught him, he took care with his appearance and dressed well no matter where he went.

"We called him 'The Cat' because of the way he dressed," said Stein. In the late 1940s, the hipster and beat movements were just beginning to stir on campuses across the nation. One particular term of affection for someone considered to be cool and with it was "Hepcat," or "Cat," and so the first time a frat buddy referred to Bob as a "cool cat" it stuck.

Word about his propensity for being a sharp dresser traveled quickly, and, before long, the girls on campus were drawn to him like a bee to honey. And he loved every minute of it.

"Boy, did he date," said Stein, "though he never dated any one girl on a steady basis. He would take a girl out one night, and then the next day I'd see him with a different girl." Did Stein notice anything that the girls he dated had in common with each other?

"They were knockouts," he replied.

Indeed, Loretta Weber, then a part-time model, dated Atkins in the summer of 1952, after he had finished his first year of med school and he returned to Dayton for a short time to visit his mother.

"He was not like the other guys," she said. "He was very handsome, and he was a real gentleman, which is not something that could be said about other men his age." Weber added that two other characteristics that made Atkins stand out from others she dated were that he was very well read, and that he was very knowledgeable about art.

But to Weber, even back then, there was one thing that made him different from the rest: "He adored his mother," she said. "He did lovely things for her all the time. He was a very loving son."

In the summer of 1951, after he graduated from college but before he enrolled in medical school, Atkins headed for the Borscht Belt in the Catskills to try his hand at comedy. His performances both onstage and as a comic waiter—where comedians of lesser talent were relegated to joking with the diners while simultaneously serving dinner with a flourish—impressed not only audiences but also a talent scout who caught his show one evening. On the spot, the scout decided that he wanted to represent Atkins and presented him with a contract at the end of the evening. Atkins was about to sign it when he happened to mention to his future manager that he was heading for medical school in the fall.

The scout, knowing all too well the unstable life of a performer, took the contract back before Atkins could sign it. "Take my advice," he told him, "go to medical school instead."

Atkins was chastened, but then he figured he could always incorporate his flair for comedy into his practice as physician. After all, the aim of both professions was to make people feel better, wasn't it?

Though Robert Atkins couldn't have envisioned the path his medical career eventually would take, as it turned out he wasn't too far off.

2.

THE THIRTY-POUND BREAKTHROUGH

At the midpoint of the twentieth century, medicine was making great technological strides. Although to those living today, fifty years later, it would appear that the medical world Robert Atkins entered when he began his study at the Cornell Medical School on Manhattan's Upper East Side was nowhere near the high-tech one today.

Into this fray stepped twenty-one-year-old Atkins, a wide-eyed, optimistic student of medicine, just like the ninety others who became members of the class of 1955. Two women were in his class, a rarity at the time. By the time he completed his studies and residency eight years later, the seeds had been planted for him to become a very different kind of physician from those that Cornell and other top-ranked medical schools liked to claim as alumni.

Ronald Arky, M.D., today the Charles S. Davidson Distinguished Professor of Medicine at the Harvard Medical School, enrolled in the same class at Cornell with Atkins. In order to keep some semblance of order among the students, school administrators arranged everything in alphabetical order, from initial seating arrangements to making clinical rounds third year. Arky was right next to Atkins in the class roster, and the two became close friends.

"He was an extrovert who was very, very quiet," said Arky. "He was really a very sensitive and caring individual, and sometimes it wouldn't come out. There was an element of shyness to him, and I sometimes wonder if that extrovert, the Jackie Mason in him, came out to compensate for an inner shyness. There were an awful lot of paradoxes about Bob." For one, he says, while Atkins was a big fish in small- and medium-sized ponds back in Dayton and Ann Arbor, New York was a brand-new ocean, and at first he felt out of place in the big city. Arky said it took Atkins some time to acclimate to the change.

Ronald Arky was also Jewish, and, along with one other Jewish student, there was a grand total of three Jews in the entire class. While administrators and professors never made a big deal out of it, Bob was caught a little off guard by the slight whiff of anti-Semitism that they occasionally perpetrated at the school. He probably thought once he became a resident of New York City, he would never encounter another person who would see his Jewishness first and him as a person second. So he had to alter his fantasies about an open-minded city and an open-minded school as well.

"Cornell wasn't exactly known for its openness for accepting Jews," said Arky, noting that none of the three Jewish students would ever challenge a professor on a topic, since although the professor may be inclined to answer the question there was a good chance that afterward he would call attention to the fact that the student was not of Gentile descent. "For instance, we wouldn't dare ask to reschedule an examination that was given on Yom Kippur," he added.

With that, the students hit the ground running from Day One. Not only did Atkins and his classmates learn about human anatomy and how the body worked, the state of medical diagnosis was nothing like it is today. As is often the case, a majority of cutting-edge medical advances are often developed in the course of a nation's most recent war, and when Atkins began medical school new techniques that evolved in the wake of World War II were just starting to become standard practice. For instance, the first open-heart surgery was conducted in 1953. To put things into further perspective, modern CPR was not instituted until the late 1950s, and the cardiogram had to be physically developed, it didn't just pop up on a monitor instantly. "To us, ultrasound sounded like Buck Rogers," said Arky. "Compared to today, medical technique was extremely crude, and instead we were taught largely to rely on the results of a physical examination and a patient's prior medical history."

While students began tagging along on clinical rounds in their second year of med school, it wasn't until the third year that they started making hospital rotations and visiting patients without the direction of a supervising physician. Again, given their last names, Arky and Atkins usually ended up on the same team, and they were often farmed out to Bellevue Hospital, the city's most notorious public hospital.

Arky remembers watching how Atkins interacted with patients. "He was very adept at taking a history and he had a good rapport with patients," he said. Other students were hesitant and clearly uncomfortable approaching patients, but Atkins liked to jump right into the fray. "Bob's manner was friendly, and he would often use a kind of self-deprecating humor with people," he added.

That is, as long as those people were lying in a hospital bed. When it came to Atkins's fellow students, aside from Arky and a couple of other students, he tended to keep to himself. In the first two years of medical school, most of the students lived in an old army barracks located on York Avenue and East 68th Street, just across from the medical school. Most of the students would congregate in small groups in the dorms and at a couple of bars and restaurants in the neighborhood in their off-hours. Atkins rarely joined his classmates on social outings. As Arky recalled, most of his excuses against socializing were that he had to study. He said that Atkins once confessed that he felt like he was in way over his head in medical school, despite the fact that he mostly breezed through high school and college. And what remained unspoken was that the last thing he would do would be to ask one of his professors for extra help and guidance, lest they unleash a Jewish slur in his direction.

On the few occasions when he did socialize with fellow students, however, he clearly stood out. "Most of us would be without a tie or a jacket when we went out," said Arky. "We had to wear lab coats all day and just wanted to relax in the evening. But Bob always showed up wearing a tie and jacket and looking pretty sharp. In relative terms, in the fifties, he was quite a fancy dresser, so I nicknamed him 'The Duke' early on." He added that Atkins considered himself to be quite the ladies man, and was constantly trying to score points with any attractive woman who happened to walk by him on the street.

In the spring of Atkins's third year in medical school, Dr. E. Hugh Luckey was appointed the dean of the medical school. As it would turn out, many years later Luckey and Atkins would share a very intimate connection: the same wife.

For the duration of the four years he spent in medical school Atkins essentially put his head down, bit his tongue when necessary, and made it through to June 8, 1955, when he graduated from Cornell University Medical College as a member of the fifty-eighth graduating class with eighty-four of his fellow students. Then it was on to residency, the four years during which he would take everything he learned in the classroom and on the hospital ward and apply it to the real world of medicine.

Many of his classmates fanned out to hospitals around the New York metropolitan area, in order to hang on to the safety net of the community they forged during medical school. If they got chewed out by a supervising physician for a particularly egregious infraction, they could get together later that same day to commiserate over their maltreatment and, with a couple of beers, shrug it off by the time the next morning's rounds rolled around. Atkins took an entirely different route and headed upstate to Rochester University to begin a residency in cardiology. Because it was an unusual choice for a first-year resident from Cornell, he had to pull a few strings and his professors had to vouch for him before Rochester would agree to take him.

But then, unlike his fellow students, instead of spending four years as a resident at the same hospital as was the custom Atkins suddenly turned up back in New York City after only a year in Rochester. Ronald Arky believes that his experience at the hospital was the spark that lit his lifelong bitterness toward the medical establishment and hospitals in particular. The exact details were fuzzy Atkins never really confided in Arky the real reason he ended his residency so abruptly, but he did hint that he had had a major fight with the head of the hospital.

The politics at most hospitals can be cutthroat in the extreme, even more so at hospitals serving as training ground for the nation's future physicians, and Atkins's frustration with what he was discovering to be the "real world of medicine" probably reached the boiling point soon after his arrival. Add to that the fact that Rochester wasn't known as a cradle of Jewish tolerance, and that medicine in the middle of the twentieth century was still predominately a Gentile profession. It's a wonder Atkins lasted as long as he did.

It could be he was just unhappy in Rochester, of course, and that its backwater quality reminded him a little too much of the Dayton he had spent his teen years yearning to escape.

The professors at Cornell couldn't have been too pleased with his behavior after going out of their way to secure the appointment for him, and Arky says that Atkins had to practice a great deal of humility until he could resume his residency at another hospital in the city. Medicine is a small world indeed, especially among school administrators and professors who yield an immense amount of power and can determine the future of a student with one stroke of the pen. Atkins must have humbled himself to the extent that he vowed never again to stoop to that level. Just as he set his course in medical school, he completed his residency at St. Luke's Hospital by keeping his head down and his blinders on. He made a decision then and there that he would never associate himself with the extremely political world of hospitals again.

After completing their residency, the vast majority of his class-mates headed to major hospitals, where they could develop their skills and network with other doctors while building up a private practice. In the beginning of their medical careers, physicians use the hospital not only to build a network of contacts and a patient base but also to receive exposure to everyday life in the world of medicine, which is far beyond what they experienced during their residency. A handful of others choose the field of research, where they could develop theories and then execute the studies that would or wouldn't confirm their theories, collecting a salary while they're at it.

Atkins chose neither. He wasn't a researcher at heart—he enjoyed interacting with patients too much—and his disastrous experience at Rochester University showed him that he was anything but a hospital toad. He took another route in 1959 when he finished up his residency: he farmed himself out as a freelance cardiologist at night while he built up his private practice during the day. He opened his practice in a small office on East 68th Street, not far from Cornell, right after he completed his residency.

To help pay the bills while he bolstered his solo medical practice, Atkins became an on-call emergency physician and would fill in for more established doctors, primarily at night. During the early years, he went on call an average of four nights a week, which didn't interfere with his own practice because he didn't schedule his own patients' appointments until late morning or early afternoon. And owing to his specialty in cardiology, he asked the services taking emergency calls to send him anyone who sounded like he was having a heart attack. He also took on a few long-term assignments with corporations, which would often employ staff physicians who would watch over the health of top executives.

At the time, this avenue was the primary way a brand-new doctor would get started in New York without being tethered to a hospital. The corporate connection also meant that Atkins would be generating regular income, so he knew that his office rent and other expenses would be paid.

Though Atkins dutifully followed the teachings of his professors in medical school and throughout his residencies, it was obvious from the path he chose that he was attracted to the unconventional. It's important to note that this was in the era of the gray flannel suit, when corporate businessmen marched in lockstep and were highly respected in the community. Atkins was clearly headed in a different direction.

Atkins may have taken on the role of a corporate physician in order to hitch his wagon to their stars, or maybe just to see what made them tick. The executives he cared for at corporations like Du Pont and AT&T grew up in a world that was the polar opposite of Atkins's: they came with pedigrees from Andover and Yale, and naturally expected success, not struggle. Atkins, of course, came from a scrappy, lower-class background where nothing was certain and only hard work would provide an opportunity—which was by no means guaranteed—to pull yourself up by your bootstraps and make something of yourself in this world.

But instead of behaving like his professors at medical school, the executives who were Atkins's patients differed in a major way: Because he was a physician and had gone through medical school, they accorded him the respect that he had never encountered before. Even though he had strayed from the conventional path, here he was working with men from privileged backgrounds who didn't look down on him, and who, in fact, looked up to him with great admiration.

Atkins knew that those physicians who favored the more conventional path regarded him as a substandard doctor—why else would he eschew the many benefits of aligning himself with a major hospital—but another factor was that he was living the life of a cowboy, a maverick charting his own course in an age when nobody knew what the term *entrepreneur* meant. Because in his soul, he was an entrepreneur at heart, determined to show everyone who had doubted him or snubbed him that he would do just fine—indeed, thrive—without them.

"He was a maverick early on, and not just in terms of weight loss," said Bernard Raxlen, M.D., who worked with Atkins in the early 1980s. "I think he always had his own ideas about the best way to do things, and I think he never quite trusted what he was taught in medical school." While his professors stressed book learning and theories, Bob preferred to learn through observation and gut instinct. "He always had his own sense of where he wanted to go, and that was to be in a position where he could encourage people to think and rethink their ideas," Raxlen adds.

There were times in the early years when Atkins would in fact seriously doubt the wisdom of the decision he had made as well as how his "different drummer" personality ruled his every move. Indeed, he spent his first years in private practice wondering if he should chuck it all and take the easy route. Treatment of his patients varied depending upon his mood on a particular day.

"I thought the more drugs I could prescribe, the better doctor I was," Atkins said of those years. "As a cardiologist, I was taught that if my patients stayed the same—they didn't get worse—that was a success."

It didn't take long for him to become thoroughly disenchanted with this approach and to begin searching for a different direction.

"He was the most focused man I've ever met," said Barbara Stinson, a nurse who worked at Boston City Hospital in the early 1960s when Atkins came up to do some postgraduate medical training there. "He was not a particularly warm man and had a tendency to be brusque, so he didn't mix well with the nurses and other doctors. He was there for one thing and one thing alone: to learn about medicine."

But even so, it wasn't exactly all work and no play for Atkins, either.

"Sometimes a bunch of doctors and nurses would go out to a restaurant after we were late getting off a particularly busy shift," said Stinson. "We'd head for a nearby restaurant to get something to eat and drink and just relax. Some of the other doctors were married, so they usually excused themselves early, but Bob was always the last doctor to leave."

She added that he sometimes became annoying, because the nurses just wanted to hang out by themselves but Bob was always still there at last call. "He flirted with all of us, waiting to see if he could talk one of us into going home with him for the night," Stinson said. "It would start out harmless enough, but he was too much of a pest, so after a few more times the nurses would head out first after a shift and head for another restaurant before the doctors even knew we had gone."

Like most doctors have experienced at one time or another, Atkins viewed patients not so much as people but as a problem that needed to be solved. During medical school, and later in his residency, instruction focused on showing students how to use the new technological advances that were entering the medical arena while tending to fall short when teaching decent bedside manner.

Most physicians eventually learn to integrate these two diametrically opposed techniques; those who don't often pursue research instead of becoming a hands-on clinician. They also tend to eschew standard hospital affiliation—almost mandatory in drumming up work for a practice—or head directly into the almost sterile practice of corporate medicine—that is, becoming a staff or school doctor—or research.

The fact that Atkins passed up the benefits of having a hospital affiliation after he completed his residency at St. Luke's meant he was unable to experience what is largely a coming-of-age for most hospital-affiliated physicians: doctors can confer with each other not only when protocol was involved but also to hash out treatment methods and get feedback on what did and didn't work with a particular patient that day.

It's almost as if Atkins deliberately chose a direction where his beliefs and theories would not be challenged by others, since he learned early on that his unorthodox ideas would be challenged and harshly criticized by the majority of his peers.

Robert Atkins also took a maverick approach to getting the word out about his practice. He quickly figured out that if he could treat corporate stars, why not go for real stars as well?

His first brush with a bona fide celebrity came in 1962 when he helped to administer an electrocardiogram for the actor Edward G. Robinson, who was overseas at the time. In the world of medicine, this was a significant technological achievement. Of course, this wouldn't be the last for Atkins.

He decided to draw on the great appreciation for art that his mother had fostered in him and started to hang out among the movers and shakers in the art world to solicit new patients for his practice. He may not have been able to afford the art displayed at the galleries where he became a regular fixture, but at least he would meet the people who could. What was pocket change for them was a month's living expenses for Atkins. By extension, he figured if they had that kind of money, they could well afford to become his patient.

Because he worked on call at night, many of his emergencies came from New York's Theater District, where the city's wealthy would head out for dinner and then take in a show. During a few of these calls, Atkins noticed that many of the worried faces in the crowd that hovered around the prone victim he was frantically trying to revive belonged to beautiful showgirls who had been performing on stage.

And so he determined that the theater world was not only a good place to troll for people with money but also for dates who were very easy on the eye and liked to have just as good a time as he did. Ronald Arky recalls a conversation he had with a classmate who had visited Atkins in New York after his practice had been open a few years. "He said when he walked into the waiting room, it was like he had entered an audition for a Broadway musical," Arky said. "All the patients were beautiful showgirls."

Of course, this segment of Atkins's market didn't necessarily have much money, but that didn't matter. He figured at least it would supply him with a steady supply of beautiful women.

One morning in 1963, as Atkins was getting ready for work, he glanced in the mirror like he did every morning, but this time he took a good hard look. He was shocked to see that he had three chins.

While he was working his way through medical school, then afterward during his residency, and then while he was building his practice, Atkins would later admit that he had lived mostly on junk food. Having graduated from high school weighing 135 pounds, when he noticed the weight gain sixteen years later he was stunned to see that he tipped the scales at 225 pounds

Atkins was still struggling to get his four-year-old practice off the ground. He continued practicing on-call medicine on a freelance basis. He continued attending social events and art exhibits to drum up business. But it had all gotten very old. He hated to set foot inside a hospital—any hospital—but he continued to network with some other young physicians at St. Luke's Hospital, where he was helping to conduct research in electrocardiography, a relatively new procedure for the time. They began toying with the prospect of joining together to open their own diagnostic clinic. It was something that appealed to Atkins, for it meant he wouldn't have to continue struggling by himself to build a practice, and he'd have other colleagues around off of whom to bounce ideas.

Being on-call also began to sour. During one late-night summons, he rushed to the side of a woman who was having a heart attack and saved her life. Instead of thanking him, however, she coldly instructed him to call her own physician the next morning. After that, he started becoming disillusioned with the direction his career was taking; he wanted to be able to "connect" with patients, not be their servant.

Atkins was now starting to hang his hopes on the proposed clinic. He continued with his on-call work, expecting to do it for only a few more months. After several months plans began to solidify, but then they got some bad news. The office that the hospital had agreed to rent to the clinic was sold, and eventually the plans were abandoned. Atkins fell into a deep depression, having counted on the new business to boost his patient load and income, at the time only twenty-five patients a week, far from sufficient for a physician to turn into a career.

On November 22, 1963, a horrified Atkins sat glued to his seat watching the news coverage of the assassination of President

John F. Kennedy on television. Like so many other Americans who were not in the mood to give thanks that Thanksgiving weekend, he nevertheless stuffed himself, mostly out of grief. Feeling utterly powerless, suddenly the image of his triple-chinned self in the mirror popped into his mind. "I felt I had to do something, anything," he said years later. "So I went on a diet."

Atkins tried a couple of the diets popular at the time, and though he initially lost a few pounds he found he couldn't stick to any of them because they made him so incredibly hungry that he couldn't focus on anything except getting something to eat to ease the hunger.

Unlike many of his colleagues, Atkins was an avid reader of professional journals and studies. In fact, close friends say that they never saw him with a novel in his hand. Instead, he devoured everything medical that came his way. After failing with standard diets, he combed through the literature looking for diets that would allow him to lose weight without going hungry. Fasting was quite popular in the early 1960s, its biggest proponent being Garfield Duncan, M.D.

Though Dr. Duncan did not possess the media savvy Atkins would later develop, he constantly emphasized in his writings that the reason why the faster ceases to be hungry after the first day or so of fasting is due to "ketosis," a state wherein so few carbohydrates are present in the digestive system that the body is forced to burn fat instead for fuel. "Ketones" are the waste products appearing in the urine when the body is in a state of ketosis and relying on stored fat.

Walter Lyons Bloom and Gordon Azar, Atlanta physicians, conducted a study that showed that ketosis could also be achieved by consuming protein and fat, but no carbohydrates, an infinitely more attractive proposition for dieting than fasting. Published in the *Journal of the American Medical Association,* their findings provided the spark for Atkins to launch his empire.

Atkins also cited a study by British researchers Dr. A. Kekwick and Dr. G.L.S. Pawan, who discovered that people who ate a diet containing virtually no carbohydrates but up to 2,000 calories per day of fat and protein would still lose copious amounts of weight. In fact, they were surprised to find that the participants lost just as much weight as those who were on a total fast, consuming nothing more than water.

Contrary to popular belief, Dr. Atkins was not the father of low-carb diets, as he was sometimes referred to. That honor belongs to a nineteenth-century British undertaker by the name of William Banting. Before he discovered a diet that reduced his top weight of 202 pounds—on a five-foot-five frame—he struggled with a plethora of weight-reduction strategies that still sound familiar to us today.

In his *Letter on Corpulence,* which was published in 1864, Banting wrote:

> Of all the parasites that affect humanity I do not know of, nor can I imagine, any more distressing than that of Obesity, and, having emerged from a very long probation in this affliction, I am desirous of circulating my humble knowledge and experience for the benefit of other sufferers, with an earnest hope that it may lead to the same comfort and happiness I now feel under the extraordinary

change—which might almost be termed miraculous had it not been accomplished by the most simple common-sense means.

Though the language is a bit stilted and formal to twenty-first-century American ears, it's not difficult to understand his point. Though obesity today is blamed on everything from television and video games to a lack of willpower, it was no less of a struggle in nineteenth-century Britain, and people who were severely overweight then were teased and ridiculed as often as people are today.

William Banting was born in London in 1796 into a family of undertakers responsible for handling the funerals of the royal family. Back then, undertakers often doubled as carpenters, since they were responsible for building the coffins used for burial.

In pre-Victorian England, obesity was a somewhat rare affliction. It's likely that most overweight people in the mid-nineteenth century belonged to upper-class families with ample means to supply a family and its servants with food. Banting entered the family business as a young adult and settled into an upper-class lifestyle typical of the time that included lots of rich food and wine and very little exercise. A diet consisted of numerous slices of buttered toast with sugared tea for breakfast; meat, pastry, beer, and more bread for lunch; a teatime repast of more buttered bread and sugary tea—Banting admitted he was very fond of bread and had at least a few slices at every meal—and a fruit tart, milk, and more bread for a "light" prebedtime supper.

By the age of thirty, William Banting was significantly overweight. By the time he reached his sixties, he weighed just over two hundred pounds, and he spent every minute of every day in extreme discomfort. Essentially he had added one pound each year of his adult life. He was so heavy that, walking down a flight of stairs, he kept his back to the staircase because the stress on his knees, hip joints, and ankles was so severe. He also wore boots and relied on a boot hook to pull them on since he was unable to bend over to tie his shoelaces.

Not that Banting hadn't tried to lose weight previously. For two decades, he checked himself into the local hospital at least once a year to avail himself of the latest medically approved weight-reduction techniques. He "took the waters" at elegant British spas, where it was recommended that he drink gallons of water smelling of rotten eggs; he sat in steam baths for hours at a time; he tried starving himself numerous times. Banting liked to row his boat on a nearby river, so once he began a serious exercise regimen of rowing for at least two hours daily. This added exertion only served to increase his appetite along with his weight. By the time he was sixty-six years old, he had also started growing deaf, so he consulted Dr. William Harvey at the Royal College of Surgeons, who specialized in diseases of the ear, nose, and throat, since his regular physician was on vacation at the time.

It was August 1862 and Banting had finally found the weight-loss method that would work miracles for him. At the time of their meeting, Dr. Harvey was marveling over a medical conference he had recently attended, where he heard a presentation by French physiologist Dr. Claude Bernard. Little was known about diabetes in Victorian times, and new research was being conducted about the ways that different foods—fats, starches, sugars—affected levels of bile in the liver, and the rest of the body as well, so Harvey was curious when Banting walked in complaining of hearing loss.

Harvey examined Banting and discovered that the cause of the hearing loss was immense deposits of fat pressing against his ear canals and eardrums. When Banting confessed his lifelong struggle with obesity, Harvey recognized a willing guinea pig. He immediately put him on the following diet:

- Up to six ounces of bacon, beef, mutton, venison, kidneys, fish, or any form of poultry or game.
- The "fruit of any pudding"—he was denied the pastry.
- Any vegetable except potato.
- At dinner, two to three glasses of good claret, sherry, or Madeira.

In addition, Banting could drink tea without milk or sugar, but champagne, port, and beer were strictly forbidden, and he could have only one ounce of toast a day, a radical change from his usual quota.

Though William Banting was clearly skeptical, he figured he had nothing (or everything) to lose, and at least he would enjoy eating foods on this diet as opposed to not eating on the other restrictive diets he had tried and that failed him. It did mean, though, he had to give up the buttered slices of bread he loved so much. To his surprise, the weight soon started to fall off, and, better yet, he never experienced the stinging hunger he had on the other diets. Though the "calorie" as a means of measuring food intake had not yet been formulated, Banting nonetheless lost eighteen pounds by Christmas 1862. The following year, he continued to lose weight, at the rate of about a pound a week, and his health improved as a result. He could hear again, he could walk down a flight of stairs again like other people, and again he could wear shoes with laces.

Though Banting continued in the family business, he now was so enthusiastic about his weight loss and return to health that he became history's first low-carb evangelist. Using the theories put forth by Harvey, Banting wrote and self-published his *Letter on Corpulence* which went on to become something of a bestseller, selling more than sixty thousand copies in England alone. Publishers from other countries soon acquired the rights, and the idea of low-carb dieting was born.

In the meantime, competitors with different ideas about dieting were conducting research to discount Banting's ideas. Or maybe, so typical today, they were just jealous of his success. The concept of calorie was first promulgated toward the end of the nineteenth century by one Wilbur Atwater, a chemist who devised the formula that one calorie equals the heat required to increase the temperature of one gram of water one degree Centigrade. He then tested a variety of foods to determine their caloric content. From there, other scientists determined how the body processes calories in terms of physical activity, in other words, how much activity equals the food energy contained in a slice of buttered bread. It's these experiments that are solely responsible for the calories-do-count attitude that pervaded the weight-loss industry throughout the twentieth century and still continues on to this day.

In the wake of the success of *Letter on Corpulence*, a California doctor, Lulu Hunt Peters, seized on the concept of counting calories and published her successful diet book *Diet and Health With a Key to the Calories* in 1917. Her book sold more than two million copies worldwide, setting the pendulum swinging in the "diet wars": when one diet is in vogue, the polar opposite diet is routinely criticized.

The next low-carb proponent was physician Alfred Pennington, who, like Atkins, pursued employment with a corporation instead of a hospital. The Du Pont Company brought Dr. Pennington on board just after the end of World War I in 1918 to help its executives lose weight. They had been following Peters's advice to the letter, but instead of losing weight they were gaining it.

Pennington, researching various weight-loss methods available at the time including their rates of success, chanced upon William Banting's treatise. He mapped out a plan that looked a lot like Atkins's later plan—restricting daily carb intake to a maximum of 60 grams, and one serving of a selection of fruits and vegetables. When the weight began to drop off, Pennington published papers on his findings in numerous medical journals.

Then there was Blake Donaldson, M.D., who, also like Dr. Atkins, was a cardiologist in New York City. While other physicians examined both the living and the dead to conduct research into the cause of obesity, Donaldson visited the American Museum of Natural History to check out the skeletons, or, more specifically, the teeth of Inuit tribe people to determine the health of people who took other than a low-calorie-diet approach for weight loss.

There were several other low-carb-diet gurus who were able to publicize their ideas in the years before Robert Atkins appeared on the scene, but they all followed the path of fad diets, making a large splash initially before petering out or being overtaken by the next big thing to come along.

After Atkins decided that a diet low in carbohydrates was something he could live with—and his research showed that it would work—he decided to give it a try. He threw out the bread and donuts in his kitchen, instead filling the refrigerator with as much fresh shrimp as it would hold. He followed the same routine when he wasn't at home.

He lost twenty-eight pounds in six weeks. The rest is history.

Most important, the whole time he didn't feel hungry at all. "It was almost as if the more I ate, the more I lost," he said.

Not only did the weight fall off him effortlessly without hunger, but Atkins also found he needed only five and a half hours sleep each night on this diet instead of the eight and a half hours he needed on his regular high-carb diet.

After Atkins lost all the weight he had set out to lose, the writing was on the wall: He decided to shift the focus of his medical practice from cardiology to weight loss. He knew there were a lot of people out there like him who wanted to lose weight without being driven mad by hunger doing it.

3.

HAPPINESS IS A PURPLE STICK

By the time New Year's Day 1964 had arrived, Robert Atkins realized that he was onto something that was almost too good to be true. He had lost twenty-eight pounds in six weeks and never felt hungry! He thought this an amazing revelation. How was it possible that no one else besides the doctors whose studies he'd read were familiar with this theory? Did they want to keep it quiet? In Atkins's eyes, everyone who struggled with weight deserved to discover it, too.

Atkins always knew he would make his mark on the world in one way or another. Would the low-carbohydrate, no-hunger approach to dieting be the ticket for him?

First, he had to try it out. It worked for him but would it work for others just as easily? While he didn't have enough patients in his private practice to try it out on—and not all of them needed to lose weight—most of the executives he treated in his position as a corporate physician at AT&T wouldn't mind losing a few pounds. Besides, as the weight slipped off Atkins in late 1963 and into the new year—as others were gorging themselves to deaden the pain of

President Kennedy's death—more than a few of the "gray flannel suits" had asked him what kind of diet he was following.

He decided to try out his low-carb experiment on a group of sixty-five of the executives, typing up a diet plan consisting of foods they could eat and those they could not. At weekly meetings, he charted their progress, listened to their experiences, and answered their questions, all the while closely monitoring their health as a regular part of the job.

At first, the executives didn't know quite what to make of the brash physician who was telling them they could eat all the steak, lobster, and butter they wanted and still be able to lose their excess pounds. After all, Richard Chamberlain's *Dr. Kildare* was more to the American taste at the time than this pushy doctor with the crazy ideas. But they figured they would at least give it a try. After all, he was a doctor, he wouldn't be advising them to do something that would harm them. And it was only for a short time. If they started to feel bad, they reasoned, they'd stop.

And then an amazing thing happened. The men who were following the diet experienced the same epiphany that Atkins had a few months earlier. Though the executives complained about not being able to eat bread or potatoes, or drink martinis in an age when the three-martini lunch was the norm—to which Atkins would nod sympathetically—they marveled at how rapidly the pounds were coming off. The best part was that these men who so prided themselves on their masculinity—some were veterans of World War II—could eat beef and still lose weight without being hungry. In the end, sixty-four of the sixty-five executives at AT&T

who had followed Atkins's diet lost all the weight they set out to lose, the sixty-fifth having lost half what he wanted to lose. Better yet, word was spreading about the miraculous diet this doctor had come up with. It didn't take long before secretaries, operators, even linemen were all losing weight without feeling the least bit hungry.

Atkins felt the results were so positive that it was time to go to the next step and let his other patients try it. Though he had tinkered with the basics during the AT&T trial run, since he had been in regular close contact with the executives and simply gave them a pep talk and other encouragement if they felt like going off the diet or just needed a friendly ear, with patients in his private practice he might not see them for months between appointments. And while he gladly took their phone calls on any medical question they might have, he didn't have enough time to answer their every question about how to maintain an ideal carbohydrate intake.

Because Atkins didn't have the time to monitor every patient so closely, he decided to advise that all patients who were following the diet purchase a box of Ketostix, thin strips of paper originally designed to help diabetics keep tabs on blood sugar levels. For the purpose of following a low-carb diet, a strip would turn purple if the body is in ketosis. In this way, recommending that patients use Ketostix to confirm that they were not eating too many carbohydrates would not only keep Dr. Atkins free to see other patients—which was rapidly becoming his favorite part of being a physician— but would also provide dieters with a way they could confirm for themselves that they were at, over, or below their ideal level of carbohydrate intake. He discovered that some patients would stop losing weight—"exit ketosis"—if they ate more than forty to fifty grams of carbohydrate per day, and, if such was the case, they could then adjust their carbohydrate intake accordingly.

From the first days when Atkins spelled out the specifics of a low-carb diet to patients in his private practice, he recommended that they use Ketostix to take control of their own weight loss. To underscore his point, just as a patient was leaving his office he often would call out: "Now remember, happiness is a purple stick!"

While he viewed Ketostix as a great motivator, Atkins also knew that he would be responsible for keeping his weight-loss patients on the diet, even between office visits. Early on, he realized that some patients—particularly young female patients—looked upon him as a kind of father figure. And so he began to develop a style of interacting with them that he believed would help them stick to the diet. It was almost as if he said to himself, "They want a father figure? Okay, I'll give them a father figure they'd better listen to!"

He began to bully them, both in his manner and in the physical layout of his office. Atkins arranged his private office so that he sat behind a massive mahogany desk that was set high on a platform. A patient would have to crane his or her neck up in order to look at him. The desk was so intimidating that when Atkins perched behind it, some patients were reminded of the Wizard of Oz. Many people would jokingly refer to it as the "Desk from Oz." Behind the desk hung deep red drapes, much like the kind that hung in the boudoirs of eighteenth-century French royalty. Placed on the side of the desk closest to the patient were numerous carved wooden figures of Hotei, the Japanese Shinto god of satisfaction and trade. With their happy faces and especially their huge stomachs, Atkins used them to warn patients, "See how fat you'll become if you don't watch your carbs!"

Atkins also liked to keep patients waiting nervously for an hour or more while listening to him chew out other patients for not producing a purple stick at the exam that day. One possibly unintentional result was that the waiting patients often resembled one big group therapy session that lasted all day, only the members were constantly changing. And while his medical staff referred to his outbursts as the "wrath of the inner office," there was a "wrath of the waiting room" as well. At times, it was little more than a bevy of elegantly dressed "ladies who lunch," engaging in a game of "Daddy likes me better than you," regardless of whether the patients had ever met before or not.

And it all hedged on whether that little paper strip had turned purple . . . or not.

Word was quickly traveling about the weird diet that worked, and—now that Atkins had a little extra money to spend he decorated the waiting room with some of the contemporary paintings that he started to acquire at Christie's and Sotheby's auction houses. Patients lounged in large, overstuffed armchairs and chatted with each other about their trials and tribulations with their diets since their last visit. Extending the psychological battle into the waiting room was all part of Atkins's desire to psych out his patients by any means possible: First, the comfortable chairs could make a patient feel lulled into a false sense of complacency about his or her impending visit with the doctor, especially if the patient had cheated on his or her diet, even slightly, since the last visit.

The waiting room wrath also intensified because Atkins found it difficult to turn away a patient, and, as a result, he was chronically overbooked. Patients who waited two or more hours were offered appointments with other physicians, but it was rare that the offer was accepted. Once patients arrived at the palace, they were going to dig in their heels and wait for an audience with the king himself, schedule be damned.

While waiting, patients discussed their entire caloric intake of the previous week in excruciating detail, obviously practicing for their audience with Atkins himself. In addition, those who had strayed often confessed in this setting. As if taking a cue from Atkins himself, those who had confessed would more often than not be shunned by those who claimed that they had spent the entire week in virtuous pursuit of a low-carb diet. One patient who first visited Atkins in 1968 said that these waiting room talks turned into marathon therapy sessions that would help to prepare them when the time came to rise up out of the easy chair and head for the inner office.

Another nod to Atkins's paternalistic nature was the "next in line" room right outside his office, where those up next could hear everything going on in the lion's den. Fran Gare tells of her first visit with Atkins and how her nervousness increased as she sat in the room.

"Through the door I heard Dr. Atkins loudly berating a patient for having gone off the diet," she said. "I heard sobbing and then a promise that she would never cheat again. When the door opened, I was amazed to see a well-dressed, extremely thin woman walk out. Her eyes were red and puffy, and, when she saw me, she nodded, as if to say, 'He's all yours.'" Gare admits that she had to restrain herself from following the woman out the door and skipping her meeting with Atkins altogether. "At the time, I weighed three hundred pounds. If he could get that mad at a woman who looked like that, what would he do to me?"

Fran Gare was too stunned to move. Atkins stuck his head out the door, looked at Gare, smiled, and stuck his hand out to her. "I'm Dr. Atkins," he said pleasantly. "Come on in."

"It was almost like he had to bully them into it," adds Fred Pescatore, M.D., who worked for Atkins in the 1990s. "He viewed himself along the same lines as a Marine sergeant, you know, berate the plebe and break him down until he finally agrees to it, although I thought that he was very selective about who he did that with. But he wasn't always right on that count, because we'd get patients who absolutely hated him."

"These are your orders," Atkins would regularly tell a patient who had fallen off the low-carbohydrate wagon. "You are commanded to follow the diet. You do not have the privilege of going off it."

To avoid losing patients altogether—even though new ones walked in the door every single day—Robert Atkins would sometimes bargain with them, because he viewed losing a patient as an absolute failure. And while Atkins would bully a patient around in the beginning, if he sensed there was a chance the patient would walk he'd tone down his delivery, and even tell patients they could eat something he had railed against during the previous visit.

"Now, let's see," he'd say to another patient, "I've been letting you eat a little melon and four slices of bread. Would you like to trade those in for something with equivalent carbohydrate next week?" he would offer.

"How about pears and cherries?" asked the patient.

"Okay, but keep the pears small," he agreed.

After all, he was their doctor, so of course he wanted people to do what he told them to do, and he tried to use a technique that he believed had the best chance of helping them to succeed. Naturally, he got a little upset when they didn't, so whenever a patient neglected to follow his plan to the letter he felt betrayed and extremely disappointed.

While Atkins had a well-deserved reputation of being loud and confrontational with many of his patients, he also cared deeply about them all, almost to the point of obsession at times. Former colleagues say he would stop at nothing to help them. To an outsider listening to Atkins scream at a patient, it sounded as though he was being anything but helpful.

"His patients were his passion," says Judy Klopp, the head nurse at the Atkins Center for fifteen years in the 1960s and '70s. "The man was a purist. He once fired a nurse for telling a patient it was okay to have oatmeal for breakfast." She contends that many people—patients and others who knew about his predilection to berate them—didn't understand the reasoning behind Atkins's behavior. "He would only yell at the patients if they cheated. He thought that they wouldn't follow the diet if he treated them nicely."

But he also had a sensitive side, especially when it hit close to home.

Klopp tells of the time when an extremely obese older man

came into the office for his initial medical exam. She was performing the standard tests and procedures before Atkins came in to see
the patient and was just about to take his blood pressure. She asked
the man, who weighed well north of three hundred pounds, to roll
up his sleeve for the cuff. That's when she saw the Nazi concentra-
tion camp number tattooed on his arm. She knew Atkins would
soon knock on the door, so instead of wrapping the cuff around the
man's bicep she excused herself from the exam room.

"I didn't always agree with the way he yelled at his patients, but
at least he'd listen to me when I told him not to do something," she
said. She cornered the doctor in the hall on his way to the exam
room. " 'No way are you going to yell at that man in there,' I told
him, shaking my finger in his face."

"What man?" he asked. Klopp told him about the tattoo.

"His face paled a little, then he entered the room and shut the
door behind him," she said, adding that she hovered near the room
during the examination to make sure that he didn't so much as raise
his voice. He didn't.

Another way he showed his soft side was every December when
Atkins threw a Christmas party and would invite all of his patients.
He asked them each to bring a potluck dish for the buffet, and, of
course, no one would dare prepare anything that didn't slavishly
follow the diet. He held the party at his office, and he always managed to squeeze in anyone who showed up.

As word spread about the Atkins diet and his private practice finally began to grow, Atkins could start to relax a little when it came

to his finances. Though he was still living in the same one-bedroom apartment he rented when he completed his residency, he began to nurture the love of art that Norma had instilled in him. Beyond shilling for patients at gallery openings, he started to learn about the art world. He even bought a few pieces here and there, even though there wasn't much wall space in the apartment. But he didn't want to collect the same kind of gauzy, Impressionist pieces that his mother did. Instead, he pursued modern art, and he began to attend auctions and have dinner with art dealers and representatives from Christie's and Sotheby's. In fact, when a particular piece he coveted was up for auction during business hours, he would often send one of his nurses to bid on it.

"More times than I'd care to remember, I'd spend my lunch hour sitting at an auction at Christie's wearing my nurse uniform surrounded by rich New Yorkers dressed in mink," said Judy Klopp.

While she didn't particularly care for the style of modern and abstract art Atkins favored, many of his colleagues regularly razzed him "for buying something that looked like a first-grader created it," as Bernard Raxlen, M.D., a colleague, put it.

"What a bunch of junk," he laughed. "And he would pay tens of thousands of dollars for this stuff." He believed there was great irony in Atkins's pursuit of art: "While Norma provided him with an informal education in art, what did it do for him? In later years, he could have taken all the money he was spending on the art and used it instead to sustain a good clinical trial where he could have doubled the life expectancy of people from the beginning. He was certainly wealthy enough, but he wasn't the least bit interested in substantiating his intuitive clinical practice with the science of good research back then."

Maybe a psychologist would attribute his interest in modern art to the little-known fact that he was a die-hard *Star Trek* fan, rarely missing an episode of the show. Though he spent so much time working and reading medical journals that he was famous for not knowing what was going on in the culture currently, even in the social and political upheaval of the late 1960s Atkins made a huge exception when it came to *Star Trek*. Shirley Linde served as Atkins's coauthor on several books. "He didn't go to conventions and he didn't get weird about it, but the only thing he did when we took a break from our sessions was to time it so he could watch *Star Trek*," she said.

Around the same time that Atkins began to build his personal art collection, he acquired his first English sheepdog. In the same way that he had earlier used the art and theater worlds not only to meet women but also build up his medical practice, Atkins probably figured that having a dog that not many other dog lovers in the city would bother with—a big, furry, drooling creature that needed constant grooming and attention—would also serve the same purpose. It helped him stand out, and perhaps even marked his practice as being different from the others, since it was a rare day when the dog stayed at home confined to the apartment. Maybe he even thought that the dog would help a patient stick to the diet, by reasoning, "Dr. Atkins may yell at me, but, with a dog like that, he can't be all bad." Occasionally, a patient would complain about the presence of a dog in a doctor's office, but, for the most part, Atkins's instincts were right.

"He really loved that dog," said Roger Rapoport, a journalist who spent time with Atkins while writing the book *The Super-Doctors*. "The first dog—named Dum Dum—was a big part of his life. Atkins was really very shy, and I think he saw a dog like that as a tremendous opportunity to get out and meet people. English sheepdogs are huge dogs, and the dog usually got more attention than Atkins did."

He added that in a whirlwind life such as the doctor was living—a constant influx of new patients, building his practice, an active social life—the dog was really the only stable fixture in his life. "He had more empathy for the dog than for anyone around him," said Rapoport. "The dog was the only family he had in New York."

Though he was naturally shy in new social situations, Atkins was a ladies' man who was active on the social circuit, serving two purposes: it would help drum up business for his fledgling practice, and it would also help him to meet women. That's how he met an editor at *Vogue*, who heard about his diet, tried it, then featured it in the magazine.

Atkins had developed a reputation as being good in bed, and, inevitably, a number of women—who may or may not have benefited from his take on weight-loss—visited the office and became his patient solely to have sex with him.

Ronald Arky recalls that Atkins would keep his friends updated on the way he learned to mix his social life with his medical practice, sometimes killing two birds with one stone. "He would often tell me he had patients who wanted to sleep with him and so they stuck to the diet just so they could get into bed with him," said

Arky. While it may have been slightly unethical, he countered when challenged on the practice, "They came to me first." Or at least it could be considered smarmy, because Atkins was not in violation of the Hippocratic oath, and because he could justify that he was indeed helping them lose weight. After the women got tired of him, however, they'd transfer their medical records to another doctor and go off the diet.

One woman who fell into that category is collecting Social Security today. Recalling those days, she said that even back then she considered Atkins to be a quack, but, like all the other women at the time, she just wanted to sleep with him. "I could always lose the weight, that wasn't the problem," she said. "I just wanted to jump his bones." And so she became a patient, went on the diet, lost a few pounds to make him happy, and then promptly went to bed with him. Afterward, she'd go off the diet because she didn't think it was healthy and the weight would come right back on.

But it also worked the other way around, where it would be he who first suggested a professional relationship turn into something more. In fact, Atkins dated so many of his patients that he came to view the line, "Call the office and let me give you a glucose tolerance test," in the same way other bachelors of the time used the line "Would you like to come up and see my etchings?"

A woman named Barbara, who served as the national spokesmodel for a national food manufacturing company for several years in the 1960s and '70s, first met Atkins when she became his patient. She was gaining weight, which threatened her position with the company, and she needed to do something about it and fast. Atkins asked her out during her second visit to his office while administering a glucose tolerance test.

Barbara brushed him off, thinking he was joking. On her third visit, he asked again, and this time she accepted. They were an item for a time, but she quickly grew tired of his philandering.

"Bob's the kind of guy that likes to check out different women," she said. "I got tired of him dating around so much, and finally I told him I wanted to be number one. He thought about it for a couple of days and finally said okay."

He lasted a week or two, until the next one came along.

While some people today may look at a picture of Dr. Atkins on the cover of his first book and wonder what all these women were making such a fuss about, it's safe to say that younger women will always be attracted to older men with money. Even though it would still be several years until his first book was published, Atkins and his swarthy good looks were considered to be a hot ticket by any number of beautiful young women, and any number of not-so-beautiful, not-so-young women as well.

The same could be said when it came to his female office staff as well, for, in addition to his patients, Atkins regularly dated his nurses. More than a few former employees described how he would decide whether or not to hire a particular woman as a nurse or assistant based on her looks. In fact, since he had the final say on hiring new employees, he'd usually base his decision on how easy on the eye they were. And if he could catch a glimpse of their ankles, so much the better.

"He liked women with nice-looking ankles," said Bernard

Raxlen, "but I always told him that his hiring criteria weren't very smart." Atkins's response was that he was well aware of that, and then sometimes he would go right ahead and get involved with the woman for a couple of weeks and then dump her, until the next attractive patient or prospective employee came along. Whenever that happened, the atmosphere around the office couldn't have been too comfortable. "But I don't do it very often," Raxlen claimed was Atkins's rationale, before he added, "Only when they are good-looking."

As more patients began to follow the Atkins diet, some of them began to wonder why they hadn't heard of the low-carb approach before. After all, there were lots of fad diets making the rounds in the 1960s, but this one was so obviously different—it worked, and it didn't leave you hungry—so why didn't more people know about it? And, more important, why weren't they hearing anything about it from other doctors? Once the word got out, however, it didn't take long for the naysayers to surface. In particular, the physicians of the patients who were seeing Atkins just for the diet were beginning to demand proof that the low-carb approach was not only effective but also healthy.

Whenever Atkins was questioned, he would point to the journals where he had first learned of the technique. The only caveat was that the studies described in the journals were conducted with a very small sampling of patients. Traditional studies demand that a large number of participants be involved over a long period of time, requiring big bucks, that only well-funded hospitals could afford to conduct. It was well known how Atkins felt toward such institutions.

Besides, his overall argument in the face of such queries was always that if it works, then it's okay. A clinically controlled trial wasn't needed to determine if people are losing weight or not. "All you need is a scale and to be able to tell when you get hungry," was his typical retort.

Atkins often invited other medical professionals to come talk to his patients and look at their records so they could see the results for themselves. He prided himself on his willingness to open his office to any physician or medical organization that wanted to learn more about what he was doing.

It was rare that someone actually took him up on the offer, and this reluctance would be a thorn in his side for the duration of his career. He maintained that his most vocal critics not only never examined his records or interviewed him, but they also totally ignored the reams of documentation that displayed his low-carb approach in a favorable light.

During these years, Dr. Atkins began to attend medical conventions on a regular basis in an attempt to learn about new techniques and procedures that, like his approach, were not condoned by traditional medicine but which were promising nonetheless. Such conferences often were sponsored by state medical or various specialty associations, and while Atkins would later be debunked by these groups, in the late 1960s some were geared toward unorthodox medical and nutritional approaches that would first start appearing on the radar screen toward the end of the 1970s.

Colleagues often said that when Atkins was at the office, if he wasn't with a patient he had a medical journal in his hand, usually the latest issue of the *Journal of the American Medical Association*—*JAMA* for short—or the *New England Journal of Medicine*. He would also comb through some of the more obscure journals of the day in an ongoing attempt to learn something he didn't already know.

In fact, he would regularly tell colleagues that he could never know enough, and that he was frustrated that he would never be satisfied with his knowledge base of any one field in medicine. And while so many physicians today and back then considered themselves to be a god to their patients, Atkins would actually tell a patient when he didn't know the answer to a question. Then he would go find it. In fact, he was thrilled whenever he didn't know something, since it provided him with yet another excuse to collect more information.

After all, enough for Robert Atkins was never enough.

Given the glittery art and theater circles Atkins traveled in, it wouldn't take long for him to attract his first celebrity weight-loss patients. Atkins's ideas would attract a national audience for the first time in 1965, when the newly thin comedians Buddy Hackett and Kaye Ballard made an appearance on *The Tonight Show*. Host Johnny Carson asked Hackett and Ballard, who were both patients of Atkins, how they had lost the weight, and they told him about an unknown Manhattan cardiologist and his unusual diet. Of course, they all made light of the more unbelievable aspects of the diet.

"You know how I lost this weight?" Hackett asked the audience. "Dr. Atkins used to call me every hour and say, 'Are you eating?'"

From that point on, word began to spread among media icons in New York as well as in Los Angeles. Editors, publishers, marketing executives, and Hollywood producers all started to hear raves about the diet from their colleagues. After *The Tonight Show* publicized the diet, *Harper's Bazaar* ran a story about it. And then, because they didn't want to appear as if they didn't have their finger on the national pulse, *Town & Country*, *Cosmopolitan*, *Mademoiselle*, even *Fortune*, all featured the diet in their pages. In fact, movie producer David Brown, the husband of renowned magazine editor Helen Gurley Brown, lost forty pounds on the diet.

Atkins learned very early on to sell the sizzle as well as the steak—along with the lobster and heavy cream—and particularly emphasized that his diet included all the foods that were supposed to be fattening and "bad" for you. After all, even back then it was difficult to get the attention of a beleaguered reporter or producer with a pitch for yet another low-calorie diet. Along comes Atkins and he's telling the world they can eat their favorite foods, never feel hungry, and they'll lose all the weight they want. It was a radical idea, and of course the media ate it up. Atkins's success was sealed simply because he had learned how to manipulate the media and perfect the art of the sound bite decades before the advent of the media coach.

"In every interview that he ever did, he would always make some kind of sweeping statement," said Arline Brecher, who first met Atkins in the early 1970s. "But that was the one thing that people knew about him. I mean, he always talked about eating steak and bacon, but if you read his book, if you really talk to him, or if you were a patient of his, he only said you *could* eat it." These foods, of course, weren't forbidden on the diet, but the reporters would set him up and egg him on in a way so that they would always end up with a quote from Atkins where he said, "Why, of course you can eat steak and bacon!"

Although he may have also told them that people on his diet also have to eat fish and chicken, vegetables, and all the other foods that he talked about, from the beginning it turned out that the media didn't care. It didn't take long for Atkins to realize that, and so, while he always enjoyed talking with reporters—and he didn't care if you were from the most obscure publication, he would still grant an interview, a trait he maintained until the week before he went into a coma—he quickly learned the kind of shorthand they were looking for and gave it to them freely. "Personally, that's not exactly how I would have presented it to the media," says Brecher, "but, then again, that's why he was who he was."

After *Vogue* ran a story about the diet in 1970, dubbing it "The Vogue Diet," it didn't take long for book publishers to begin circling so they could capitalize on this radically new diet that was starting to get lots of buzz around the country.

Atkins's first offer came from Bantam Books for the paperback rights, a direct result of a chance meeting that the company's chief executive, legendary publisher Oscar Dystel, had with an acquaintance who had lost a hundred pounds with Atkins acting as his physician.

Dystel offered Atkins an advance of $30,000 for the paperback rights—a huge sum back then—which, after first conferring with his lawyer, Atkins accepted. While the doctor wasn't schooled in legalese, at the time he would have signed any contract if it meant that his ideas would get a wider audience.

They teamed him up with Ruth West, a freelance writer, and the instructions were simple: Write for the lowest common denominator. In other words, forget about aiming the book at the medical experts. Make it informal, and don't even bother with footnotes or a bibliography—both mandatory when writing on most medical topics.

Initially, Atkins disagreed. "I thought this documentation would enhance the book's reception in the medical community," he said. "But the publisher told me, 'This isn't a medical book, it's a popular book that will be bought by people who don't normally read books. You're not trying to reach the medical profession.'"

Eventually, Atkins agreed, but, in retrospect, it could have been the omission of medical citations in the first edition of the book that caused the medical establishment to turn against Atkins from the very beginning.

In what was a reversal from how most book deals are conducted today, early buzz was so good on the book that after Atkins sold the paperback rights he then sold the hardcover rights to David McKay, a medium-sized publisher with a reputation for producing controversial books, as it had also published the notorious *Everything You Always Wanted to Know About Sex but Were Afraid to Ask*, by Dr. David Reuben. The hardcover edition of *Dr. Atkins' Diet Revolution* appeared in print first, in September 1972. By the time new year's rolled around, more than two hundred thousand copies were in print, and, four months after publication, the book had sold almost a million copies in all.

*   *   *

Even though Robert Atkins was on the verge of becoming the next big thing, keep in mind that, unlike a lot of the other celebrity doctors, past and present, he loved to see his patients more than anything else. In addition, he was a classically trained M.D., unlike many of the medical and nutritional experts these days who receive mail-order degrees in naturopathic medicine or nutrition and then proceed to write books that will allow them to make a career of speaking engagements.

Atkins came from a very traditional medical background, with nothing that would have suggested that he would want to buck the establishment and become a radical. "If anything," says Kurt Greenberg, a former patient in the 1980s who kept in touch with Atkins through the years, "he was the kind of guy who would very much go along with it."

But all that was about to change.

4.

The Brickbats Fly

The early 1970s were a tumultuous time in the United States. The country was polarized by Vietnam, the civil rights and women's movements, by Richard Nixon and the Watergate crisis, and by the emergence of the youth counterculture. The music was angry, the headlines were angry, and neither side could tolerate the other. Into this fray stepped Dr. Atkins with the publication of his first book, adding his own acerbic voice to the mix.

Most thought his ideas were laughable, along the same lines as the reducing machines that promised to melt pounds and inches with little more than a four-horsepower engine and a vibrating belt. Others, perhaps veterans of the chalky, foul-tasting diet shakes and potions that family physicians often prescribed then, figured that even though the Atkins diet sounded too good to be true it was worth a shot. The book soon topped the bestseller lists, stealing media attention away from other physicians and experts who had diets and nutritional programs of their own to promote.

The publication of *Dr. Atkins' Diet Revolution* in the fall of

1972 would ensure that 1973 would be the busiest year that Atkins had seen so far in his forty-three years. For not only did the book bring a host of new patients to his practice—and people would literally fly in from all over the world to become his patient—but he quickly became a doctor in demand in his office, in his social life, and particularly in the media.

The book and ensuing publicity brought even more critics out of the woodwork, along with those who now viewed things with dollar signs in their eyes, as they perceived Robert Atkins and his newfound fame as an opportunity to make a quick buck or two.

The first few months after the book was published was the sweet spot for Atkins. After all, he agreed to do the book so it would attract a wider audience to his ideas. He thought it would sell a few thousand copies in hardcover, then a few more in paperback, and he'd be done with it.

"I didn't think I'd make any money on it," he admitted.

So when the public's reception to *Diet Revolution* was so overwhelmingly positive—at one point, in January 1973, the book was selling 100,000 copies a week—Atkins allowed himself to dream a little about what could come next. His publisher would undoubtedly want him to do a follow-up book, since bestsellers were few and far between for the small publisher and Atkins had already earned tens of thousands of dollars beyond the advance that he had received.

Plus, women were literally throwing themselves at him in the wake of his huge success. While he wouldn't have minded if they became a patient of his first even if their main intention was to have sex with him, Atkins seemed to welcome all comers as long as they were young and pretty. This availability of women also applied to nurses who wanted to come to work for the famous diet doctor. Though Atkins had long used his position to hire and fire nurses based on their appearance, once he became famous he really took advantage of the situation. After all, his lifelong feeling that no matter how much he had it would never be enough also clearly applied when it came to women.

"At that time, women for him were just the chase, and he didn't talk much about the individual women themselves except in terms of jumping their bones," said Bernard Raxlen. "He was pretty chauvinistic that way. They were the prey and afterward he would discard them, which is awfully hard if you are hiring that person to integrate them into your staff."

Raxlen says that because Atkins was naturally charming and funny, he often unintentionally misled people into thinking he felt close to them. "He had what he would call friends in the art scene and some medical colleagues, but I don't think anyone really got very close to Bob," he said, adding that he felt the same way. "Over a period of time, we spent a lot of time together working on the practice, and I thought I had a very personal relationship with him, but in reality, we didn't. For many years, he disappointed a lot of people because of his lack of intimacy and commitment."

The first clue that his instant fame wasn't all it was cracked up to be came in the spring of 1973.

The Medical Society of the County of New York held a press conference on March 14, 1973, to denounce the Atkins diet, and the news made headlines across the country.

Then, several days later, the American Medical Association published a paper that specifically criticized Atkins and his low-carb diet. The standard protocol for preparing such a paper—which were often widely promoted in the media—included a close examination of the work in question and all studies and papers cited in the book, as well as others published through the years that could shed some light on the topic at hand.

In Atkins's eyes, the AMA paper studiously ignored the wealth of studies and reports that supported the low-carb thesis. Essentially, the paper said that the doctor was fudging his own results, and that he was essentially putting words in the mouths of his patients, as quoted in the book.

The AMA has always been highly respected in the medical community as well as by laypeople who closely follow medical developments and studies, and, as such, the attitude toward the organization is that once they hand down their opinion it's as good as law. In other words, like the U.S. Supreme Court, don't even try to question their conclusions because it would be futile.

Atkins was livid. All the proof he had submitted in the form of patient records, consensus letters from other doctors whose patients had similar results, and the medical studies that confirmed his findings—even the studies that Atkins had cited in the book were published in the AMA's own official journal, *JAMA*—was for naught. Though they might sometimes disagree with him, he had not expected people he thought were his colleagues to rake him over the coals in public. For Atkins, that was the last straw.

His response was fast and furious. "This is another example of the AMA's persistence in trying to force obese individuals to continue their eating patterns despite the common sense observation of every dieter that sugars and starches are fattening," he said. "I think the AMA did not do their homework because they did not do any original studies. Their studies were not done on this diet but on diets which were dissimilar."

Worst of all, he believed they weren't showing their full hand. "I felt the AMA was operating with a hidden agenda, which had nothing whatsoever to do with being scientifically on target," he said. "I could never pinpoint what it was, maybe it was self-interest, but it wasn't interest in the patients."

He marked that day as the point where he became a maverick.

"I really thought when the book came out all the medical people who saw things my way would come to the fore," he said. After all, if the so-called medical establishment automatically disbelieved facts and thousands of instances in which a person's life improved under his care, then he would do the same. Why shouldn't he question every other report or statement issued by the medical establishment?

And so, armed with an absolute venom and a feeling that the world—at least the powers that be in the world of medicine—had it in for him without ever giving him a chance, he set out to find their biases and prejudices in medical studies and findings, and, by taking the opposite approach, he'd work to prove them wrong every step of the way.

He'd get a chance to add more fuel to his fire one month later, and, this time, it would involve the federal government taking the same side as the AMA.

On April 12, 1973, Atkins appeared before the Senate Committee on Nutrition and Human Needs, which was chaired by Sen-
ator George McGovern. The committee was conducting a series of
hearings on the state of nutrition in the United States at the time,
including everything from school lunch programs to the meat industry to, of course, weight-loss programs.

This was barely six months after *Diet Revolution* was published.
When Americans turned on their televisions that night to tune into
the evening news, most reports on the Senate hearing zeroed in on a
beleaguered-looking Atkins becoming increasingly agitated at the
senators' questions. It may have appeared as though Atkins had been
subpoenaed to appear at the hearing to defend his diet, but the little-
known truth is that he had gotten wind of the hearing scheduled on
amphetamine abuse and sent a letter to the commissioner of the previous congressional session asking to speak at the hearing, since he
had lots of experience with people who had abused amphetamines for
weight loss. News reports did nothing to reveal the real reason for
Atkins's testimony and instead focused on the showdown between the
senators and the physician with the unorthodox way to lose weight.

The media wasn't entirely vicious to Atkins and his diet, however. Whenever he appeared on the wholly congenial talk shows of
the day—such as *Mike Douglas* and *Merv Griffin*—his hosts were
generous, almost brownnosing to a fault, which was generally the
style of talk shows back then.

While some reporters had benign motivations for interviewing
Atkins, others undoubtedly knew from the beginning they'd take
an antagonistic stance. While Atkins could be pretty calculating in

his dealings with the media, he could occasionally be pretty naïve and forget he was talking to a reporter.

Roger Rapoport spent time with Dr. Atkins in the summer of 1974 to interview him for *The Super-Doctors*, a book he was writing about popular celebrity doctors. He met briefly with Atkins first in his Manhattan office, and then the doctor invited him out to a house he was renting in the Hamptons for the weekend so that they could continue the interview. Rapoport noted that none of the other doctors he profiled for the book—a stellar list that included Benjamin Spock, Christiaan Barnard, and Jonas Salk—had invited him to take a more intimate look.

"I was surprised he invited me for the weekend," said Rapoport, "but I think he did it because he genuinely was a pretty friendly person, plus, he liked the attention." He believed that Atkins trusted him, but he also sensed that there was an ulterior motive in play. "He obviously felt if I spent more time with him I would write a better story, which would do a good job of promoting his work and the diet."

Some of the things Atkins revealed to Rapoport were surprising, simply because a reporter with a preconceived negative view of his diet could clearly have used the extra information as ammunition to bolster an argument against him. But Atkins took the chance, even though he knew little about the book project other than that it would be published by Playboy Press. Or, he felt the exposure by the publisher would increase his appeal to women even more.

During one conversation about the diet, Atkins let it slip that a reason why his diet was great was that he could have orange juice with his bacon and eggs for breakfast every day. His female companion for the weekend seemed genuinely shocked by his admission. She told him, "No you can't, it's not on your diet," to which he replied, "I have a swig or two."

If Rapoport had been writing for the *National Enquirer*, this would have obviously been the lead story: "Diet Doctor Cheats On Own Diet." But, then again, Atkins may have revealed his human side quite intentionally, since he knew his words would be buried in a five-thousand-word profile that would be read primarily by ultramasculine, red-blooded American men who weren't familiar with the details of Atkins's diet, and didn't give a hoot about losing a few pounds. Or if they did know about the diet, they figured, What's the big deal? The guy's human, so he doesn't follow his own diet all of the time. And this was in the days before reporters would routinely dig around in transcripts and archives looking for even a tiny damning bit of news.

"I have almost no willpower," Atkins admitted. "In fact, I'm the kind of guy who will ask the waiter for something to eat while we're being served."

And so the slip got by without making headlines across the country, which would be inconceivable today. It showed that Atkins was extremely savvy when it came to dealing with the media from the very early days of his notoriety. So when he was away from the media spotlight, but still eating in public where somebody hell-bent on outing him could easily find him, he tended to relax.

One former associate recalls that they had to constantly be on the lookout for people hovering around the restaurant table to see exactly what was on the doctor's plate, whether they could point a finger and say, "See, even he can't stick to his diet!" This same person suspects that some of his enemies bribed restaurant chefs and staff to provide a complete report of everything that Atkins ordered and ate while dining at their establishments.

The critics didn't have to look far. Besides the orange juice remark, he provided them with lots of opportunities.

Kurt Greenberg said he would often show up at a dinner at a convention or trade show where Atkins would be dining. He said that while some people would say, "Look, he doesn't even follow his own diet," he knows through years of doing business with doctors that it's the rare physician who follows his own plan even a majority of the time. "I was very idealistic and still am," said Greenberg. "I eat a very healthy organic diet and take tons of supplements, but the doctors weren't that into it. At first, I thought they were hypocrites but then I kind of mellowed out." He believed that a doctor eating a diet different from the one he is promoting to the public at large is not the point, though most people get stuck on the hypocrisy and go no further. "There's a bigger picture here," said Greenberg. "If he wrote a good book and this is what he said, but he doesn't follow it all of the time, it doesn't mean that it doesn't work. It just means that he doesn't do it."

While he admits that this is not necessarily the norm for doctors who are public figures, pushing a particular diet and suing other physicians and diet experts who publicly don't agree with them, he felt that Atkins wasn't a two-faced liar, only that when he was traveling and in the company of other doctors he relaxed a little.

"Some of the doctors are really into their diets one hundred percent, but others get up on the podium and give their speeches and then they go and eat and drink everything in sight," he noted. "I never saw it with Dr. Atkins. I just saw him eating some bread and pasta and other foods that didn't conform to his dietary recommendations, but he didn't go crazy like the others, it just meant he was off his diet."

He may not have gone off his diet just at medical conventions. In the 1980s, Betty Kamen remembered that sometimes Atkins's appearance would signal that he was obviously not following his diet.

"We were concerned because he was overweight and he really did not take care of himself," she said. "If you are on a really good diet, you are not overweight and you don't look the way he looked. He never looked healthy. We always had the feeling, unfortunately, that he didn't walk his talk, which was too bad." Like Greenberg, Kamen was able to view his diet with regard to the bigger picture. "We forgave him because he was doing so much good for so many people, and sometimes people who are caregivers neglect themselves because they are so busy caring for others."

Just as he often admitted he didn't know the answer to some patients' questions, Atkins liked to share the spotlight with other medical experts, just in case a reporter asked a question that he couldn't answer. As his fame grew, he was always open to having other doctors appear with him on radio and television shows and participate in interviews with newspaper and magazine reporters. He thought that by having a cross-section of physicians—especially if they hailed from prestigious institutions of traditional medicine—his ideas would automatically be bolstered in front of a skeptical public and therefore make them more likely to be accepted.

The thorough reading of medical journals would help immensely when his diet was questioned. He learned of the work of H. J. Roberts, M.D., whose articles in medical journals from the early 1960s suggested hyperinsulinism was caused by excessive intake of sugar and other simple carbohydrates. But Atkins waited until he had a good reason to call on Dr. Roberts. That moment arrived in 1973 when television producers were clamoring for him to appear on their shows in the wake of the roaring success of *Diet Revolution*.

Atkins contacted him while Roberts was attending a medical convention in Philadelphia. As Dr. Roberts put it, "He wouldn't take no for an answer," even though it meant an inconvenient detour for the doctor and his wife. The couple traveled to New York for the taping, they compared notes at dinner afterward, and they remained colleagues until Atkins died.

Despite Atkins's efforts to placate his critics and influence the media, he wasted no time in making enemies, whether he intended to or not, an unfortunate trait that would last for the rest of his life. Sometimes they were enemies simply due to their alignment with the naysayers who would automatically condemn anything that came out of Atkins's mouth or from his pen.

Author Arline Brecher fell into this category: she was Dr. Neil Solomon's ghostwriter on several of his books. Solomon didn't agree with Atkins's ideas or diet, which meant that Brecher also automatically denounced Atkins by virtue of her position in the opposition's camp.

"And that's how I heard about Bob Atkins," she said, "because Neil and Bob were constantly at each other's throats, going at it on every radio show where the two of them could get booked at the same time. So of course I was totally in Neil's corner."

Though they never quite broke out in fistfights, there was no love lost between Atkins and Solomon. They weren't any kinder to each other off the air than on the air, and according to Brecher, they both thought the other was an ignorant fool. "They made no pretense at hiding their disgust for each other," she added.

While Solomon served as an adviser to various state and federal governmental agencies during this time, his trajectory rapidly plummeted in the late 1970s and he disappeared from public view.

After Solomon, Atkins turned to the next opponent who could provide him with the best fight, and therefore the best media exposure. Atkins had learned that print media, radio, and TV producers just loved a good argument on camera or on the air. The sooner he could find his next worthy adversary, the better.

In fact, he was quickly discovering exactly how the media would manipulate guests and topics in order to increase the chances of having a knock-down, drag-out fight happen within view of the cameras. And this became crystal clear when Nathan Pritikin appeared on the scene.

There was no love lost between Atkins and Pritikin, whose first book, *The Pritikin Program for Diet and Exercise*, was published in 1979 and advocated an ultra–low fat diet. The sparks flew whenever they appeared together on a TV or radio show, just as they did on the *Tomorrow Show* with Tom Snyder in 1981. It took only seconds after Snyder introduced the guests for them to head straight for each other's jugular.

Atkins started things off by saying, "If people want to go on Mr. Pritikin's diet and eat beans and peas to lose weight, that's fine, you see, if that's the way they want to do it."

Pritkin hurled back that his diet included salmon, soufflés, stir-fried steak, and a chocolate mousse recipe that was even better than regular chocolate cake, to which Atkins retorted, "We don't need recipes, we can go to a restaurant and order fish, brisket, and lobster in melted butter."

Things quickly went downhill from there. The show ended with each side summarizing his position and Atkins was invited to go first. When it was Pritikin's turn, Snyder actually had to put his hand over Atkins's mouth so that Pritikin could finish talking.

After the show was over, Atkins served Pritikin with court papers for a five-million-dollar lawsuit, charging the no-fat proponent with libel and slander. "I was a gentleman," Atkins said at a news conference the following day. "I waited until the show was over."

Though Atkins and Pritikin were indeed bitter enemies onstage and off, both obviously recognized the value of controversy with a televised fight. They would continue to lock horns in front of millions of people on a regular basis because they knew that thousands of books on both sides would sell as a result. One TV producer said their joint appearance was just as good a show as a previous program that paired the Reverend Jerry Falwell with *Penthouse* publisher Bob Guccione.

In fact, one producer admitted to keeping the two separated in different dressing rooms before the show to increase the tension and therefore the entertainment value. "We were hoping for controversy," she said, "and, basically, they both made each other look like asses."

Besides Nathan Pritkin, competition from other physicians with diet books to promote didn't take long to develop. Doctors and authors pushing everything from alcohol to sex as the primary ingredient in weight loss made the rounds of the media and book signings trying to edge Atkins off his throne. Diet books that were fighting for attention at the time included *The Lover's Diet*, by Dr. Abraham Friedman, who advised people to get thin with sex. His motto: "Reach for a mate instead of a plate." He also had a diet to recommend, of course, along with the regular bedroom workouts, but he steadfastly reminded the public that one round of sexual intercourse burned an average of two hundred calories. *The Lover's Diet* faded quickly from the scene. No one else was considered a serious enough threat until a doctor in Scarsdale, New York, appeared on the scene with a prescribed eating plan that was essentially a variation on Atkins's low-carb plan only with higher levels of protein and a weekly meal schedule.

When Dr. Herman Tarnower developed what later came to be known as "the Scarsdale Diet," he was a cardiologist like Atkins, and he also traveled in one of the New York metropolitan area's highest social stratospheres: Westchester County. Like Robert Atkins, he was still a confirmed bachelor at the age of sixty-nine when his book, *The Complete Scarsdale Medical Diet*, was published in January 1979. There was little difference between the diets except that the Scarsdale was lower in fat, and it provided something new to dieters who had tried the Atkins approach a couple of times but needed the extra structure of being told exactly what to eat for each meal each day of the week.

The success of Dr. Tarnower's book kept Dr. Atkins on the defensive, against a plan that he considered merely the latest incarnation of his own. But Tarnower's fame lasted only a year, eclipsed in March 1980 by a different sort of notoriety when he was found shot to death in his home in Purchase, New York. Though he once complained that he would always be known as the Scarsdale Diet doctor, the arrest and subsequent conviction of his lover, Jean Harris, and her own well-touted escapades through the legal system, would see him upstaged.

It didn't take long for yet another tall, broad-shouldered, opinionated Manhattan physician to appear on the scene with a new diet. Dr. Stuart Berger was a Manhattan psychiatrist who treated people for food and drug addictions, and his weight-loss theory revolved around allergies that weakened the immune system and increased the tendency to gain weight.

The Southampton Diet, published in 1981, was based on the concept that once people stopped eating foods that caused even a slight allergic reaction, they would not only lose weight but their physical ailments would disappear. Berger's book sold well, but it wasn't until four years later when his next book, *Dr. Berger's Immune Power Diet*, appeared that his popularity—and a few new ideas—spiked off the charts. He explained that people develop allergies to foods they eat most often, that before long the body starts to regard these foods as "toxic," which stresses the immune system and increases one's tendency toward obesity.

People following Berger's diet first identified foods they were allergic to and then replaced them with unprocessed foods, as well as a substantial regimen of vitamin and mineral supplements. This approach was so similar to Atkins's low-carb prescription that Atkins himself provided a blurb for the jacket of Berger's book.

There were other similarities. Like Atkins, Berger grew up Jewish with parents who owned a small business and had a home life that revolved around food. He, too, attended a prestigious medical school, the Harvard School of Public Health, and became disillusioned with medicine as traditionally practiced. He felt that the way medicine was taught was a couple of generations behind the times. And he was also a longtime confirmed bachelor.

Like Robert Atkins, Stuart Berger referred to himself as a "well-adjusted workaholic." But that's where the similarities ended. Though Berger claimed that he saw as many as sixty patients a day—much like Atkins—he also claimed he would gladly give up his practice to become a celebrity psychiatrist full-time, nonetheless bristling at news accounts that he was a "media shrink."

"My sitting on *Donahue* will help far more people than if I sit in my office treating them on a one-to-one basis," Berger said. While Atkins would regularly refer to "the Center" and his goal as "his baby," Berger once used the phrase "It's like my child" to describe his newly acquired Rolls-Royce Silver Shadow II.

In 1981, *The Beverly Hills Diet*, written by actress Judy Mazel, became wildly popular. Her program prescribed a specific food regimen consisting primarily of fruits; the book jacket, in fact, featured a golden pineapple. Mazel said the diet was based on combining foods, that by eating specific foods at the same meal weight loss would be hastened. In reality, eating nothing but fruit for the first ten days of the diet was probably responsible for the claimed average weight loss of ten to fifteen pounds over a period of thirty-five days.

These diets provided Atkins with competition for a while, but they soon dropped from sight. While in the public eye, however, the majority of the physician-authors advocated something that Atkins soundly denounced and that was affiliation with a hospital, not that any New York area hospital would have anything to do with him, given his stature as a lightning rod for controversy. In the eyes of Atkins's worst critics, it was his greatest weakness.

Later, colleagues expressed puzzlement over Atkins resistance, yet he never justified it.

"One of the reasons he said he didn't need a hospital was that he wouldn't take any emergency night calls," said Bernard Raxlen. "So he would tell a patient to stay with her current doctor whether he was a cardiologist or a neurologist. He felt what he was doing was simply augmenting the program offered by the patient's primary physician." Raxlen said that Atkins advised any patient already with a doctor not to continue with any round of prescriptions that doctor may have prescribed. In his later books on nutritional healing, he made a big show of the fact that many of his patients could literally throw their pills away after signing on with him.

But advice in a book—at least back then—was one thing; contradicting the advice of a patient's primary care doctor was another. So many doctors told their patients to stop seeing Atkins—or, at the very least, get off the low-carb diet he recommended—when they found out he was telling them to stop taking their medications, and Atkins definitely didn't want any lawsuits, especially from other physicians. He was smart enough to know not to cut a patient off from his or her world of orthodox medicine. But with the kind of practice Atkins ran, he didn't need a hospital in the same way a more traditional physician did.

Atkins always maintained that he was a clinician at heart and not a researcher. He freely admitted that he didn't have a clue how to conduct a research study, and, in later years, once he began to fund a few studies out of his own pocket, those in charge had to spell out for him exactly how to plan such studies, the best protocols and controls to use, and so on.

But in the 1970s, he still vehemently maintained that the most important part of medical treatment was how a patient looked and felt, and how his or her health improved, not what some study had to say about a question initiated by the study itself in the first place. It was almost as if Atkins were a high school student who didn't want to go through all the effort of proving a theorem in geometry: Why does angle A equal angle B? His answer would have been "Because to my eye, they are the same," pointing to the illustration of the theorem in the geometry textbook.

"To my mind, the weakness of orthodox medicine is the demand for proof," he once said. "Because they have insisted on demanding proof, the area of innovation in treatment and diagnosis is not claimed by orthodox medicine. Complementary medicine believes that the truth must be determined at the time the patient walks into the office, not . . . after the patient has died."

Despite the fact that Dr. Atkins was pulled in infinitely more directions than he had been before *Diet Revolution* was published, his desire to keep an eye out for the next opportunity continued unabated, especially when it came to women. Even with his grueling schedule, he still found ample time to pursue New York's most desirable, and as many as possible. Numerous colleagues commented on his seemingly prodigious sexual appetite—it seemed that the more he had, the more he needed. As in other areas of his life, he could never get enough.

Although he was well known for womanizing, Atkins was careful to keep his political leanings a secret. He was a Republican, and though some people saw this as running counter to his chosen avocation of helping people, overall, the field of medicine tends to attract those who lean toward the right. Like other people, physicians don't much like the idea of government interference—and they want the freedom to choose the best of treatments for their patients.

In Atkins's case, his political bent derived from the intrusive policies of the FDA and other governmental agencies. "Everything about politics, in his view, stemmed from this opinion," said Kurt Greenberg. "Atkins took the traditionally Republican stand of wanting less government regulation, simply because it was a constant in his medical life."

Atkins was not fond of spending time alone, whether at work or leisure. He tended to pack his schedule so fully that by the end of the day, when it was time for sleep, and if he didn't have a young woman to spend the night with, he walked in the door of his apartment, peeled off his clothes, and fell into bed until the next morning. Then he would start up all over again with his standard bacon-and-egg—and orange juice—breakfast at a neighborhood coffee shop. Though Atkins advised his patients that the best way to follow a low-carb diet was to prepare as many meals as possible themselves, the truth is that he rarely cooked for himself, preferring to eat out instead.

In the summertime, he loved to surround himself with people of both sexes, the younger the better, and if they worked in show business or another glamorous or exotic field, better yet. In the early 1970s, he had become fond of a popular hobby among the Manhattan elite: spending the weekend in the Hamptons. While some shared houses or bought timeshares in order to hobnob with the rich and famous, Atkins liked to rent a house for the season and then cherry-pick the people who he wanted to share it with. And the fact that his Southampton house, known as the "Reeves Estate," rented for $10,000 for the season and had thirteen bedrooms and a kitchen that spanned four rooms, meant that he had to spend a lot of time finding people to share it with.

But this was something he loved to do, and in the summer of 1974 his roommates included the man who wrote the music for *Grease*, an actress who had appeared in the Broadway production of *Jesus Christ Superstar*, the former mistress of the Shah of Iran, and numerous aspiring actresses, models, and flight attendants, all of whom were young, pretty, and single. And he often told his room-mates to invite their friends, which only increased his pickings.

Of course, the girls he brought out for the weekend weren't crazy about his version of *The Dating Game*, but most would com-fort themselves that they were with him for the time, though reports of wild parties fueled with cocaine and sex—along the same lines as Hugh Hefner and his soirees at the Playboy Mansion—were leg-end. In fact, Atkins fancied himself to be in Hefner's league, and nothing much happened to disavow him of the notion.

Howard Shapiro, M.D., a Manhattan-based diet doctor, and Robert Atkins often traveled in the same circles. Though Shapiro didn't agree with Atkins's low-carb approach, he was amazed at his ability to attract the most beautiful women. A colleague once asked Shapiro if he could fix up Atkins for an upcoming bar mitzvah they were both planning to attend.

"I asked a friend who was a model if she was interested, and she said yes," said Shapiro. "I was surprised, because she was a young, very beautiful model, and I just didn't get the connection. She ex-plained that she thought it would be a very interesting experience and left it at that."

Fame and big bucks, of course, have always paved the way for young beauties to be attracted to older men who, while they may have charisma, don't necessarily have the looks to accompany it. But Atkins accompanied the young woman to the bar mitzvah, and other guests treated him like the bona fide celebrity he was.

"He stayed for the entire evening, and, all night long, people went over to talk to him," said Shapiro. "It was like having Barbara Walters come to your kid's bar mitzvah, he was that big."

As for the girl Shapiro fixed up with Atkins, from what he heard that was the only time Atkins went out with her.

After the royalties from *Diet Revolution* started to roll in, it was almost as if someone opened the floodgates on his passion—some might say addiction—to collecting art. As was the case with girlfriends, Atkins felt that he could never have enough art. And not just any art, but paintings by top artists of the day, as well as the long-deceased, which meant that the art he displayed on the walls of the one-bedroom apartment where he still lived in 1974 was a veritable mix-and-match gallery. Abstract was displayed next to Cubist, Cubist next to Impressionist. According to Roger Rapoport, the combination of styles, and the fact that paintings were hung so close together one couldn't even see the color of the wall, was extremely disorienting.

"The walls were crammed from floor to ceiling with originals by Ben Shahn, Reginald Marsh, Thomas Hart Benton, and dozens of other painters from various schools," he said. Atkins mentioned to him that he spent about forty thousand dollars each year on art, and that was in 1974. Atkins had amassed over four hundred paintings in his collection, and because he couldn't display it all in his apartment he stored some in the closets, hung some at the office, and loaned some out to ex-girlfriends and to his mother and father.

In time, it was clear that he had moved on from the gauzy Impressionist paintings his mother favored, and he admitted that he was actively looking to sell those remaining in his collection.

Unlike other people who thought that Atkins was interested in art solely for the status it afforded him, Roger Rapoport got the impression that he truly liked and appreciated the pieces. "I think he thoroughly enjoyed it because he thought it was beautiful," he said. "Plus, the art world was a great place to meet new people, he met all these amazing talented people from all over the world."

But Bernard Raxlen felt differently. "He didn't even like the stuff," he said, adding that he felt Atkins bought so many pieces of art because it was something else he could conquer in a time when it seemed that half the world was against him.

Unfortunately for Atkins, things would only get worse—far worse—before they got better.

After the success of *Diet Revolution*, however controversial, his publisher wanted lightning to strike twice. Like most physicians who write books, Atkins didn't do the actual writing himself. He worked with a series of ghostwriters, which was arranged through his publisher, editor, and literary agent, though, as was the case with hiring and firing his medical staff, he had the final say. None of his coauthors would comment on whether he used attractive ankles as his criteria for rubber-stamping a writer, but it's safe to say that since those he ultimately worked with were more familiar with the publishing process than he was he would demur to their experience. Besides, the ghostwriters usually were able to meet with him only occasionally due to his breakneck schedule of patients, publicity, conventions, and women.

When writer Shirley Linde was introduced to Atkins as a possible coauthor for what would become *Dr. Atkins' Super Energy Diet,* the first book, *Diet Revolution,* had been out for just about a year and people were coming out of the woodwork trying to get a piece of him. As a result, he was starting to become a bit more guarded in his dealings and relationships with people who knew him only as a famous diet doctor.

The two "interviewed" each other a number of times to determine if they would be a good match. Linde's primary concern revolved around Atkins's scientific credibility, since she was well aware of the controversy that swirled around him at the time. In turn, he was trying to size her up, to see if she could handle the job of working with him. After all, he had already dug in his heels with the AMA, as well as with a bunch of United States senators, so if she thought he was going to budge on his theories she had another thing coming.

Matching up the physician with the right ghostwriter can be a difficult job, since doctors are notorious for providing either too little or too much information, and they can be difficult to get in touch with given their schedules. So after a number of meetings at his Manhattan office and out in the Hamptons, Shirley Linde became frustrated that Atkins still wouldn't commit to bringing her on as his coauthor, since she clearly wanted the job. During one meeting in the Hamptons, they were sitting on the grass playing with his dog, Bumbles, and idly chatting. Said Linde, "The dog was licking me to death, so I said, 'Bob, if your dog loves me this much how bad can I be?'" Atkins agreed, and they got down to work.

While Linde clearly admired Atkins and his work, and his ability to stand up to his critics, once the work began Linde saw firsthand how Atkins's never capitulating when it came to his beliefs could be difficult to negotiate.

"He was brilliant and articulate and his patients loved him," she said. "But he always wanted things his way, so sometimes we didn't agree about what should be in the book, so we had to thrash it out, which could take days."

Mostly they worked with a tape recorder, with Linde asking questions about a particular issue which Atkins would answer, and, if he was too busy to meet in person, they would instead talk on the phone. "Sometimes he would just talk about his ideas," she said, "while other times he would get really specific and divulge patient histories or summarize scientific research." And always he would provide her with dozens of articles that had appeared in a wide variety of medical journals that she would use for background material.

According to Linde, Atkins's brain was always going a million miles a minute, and it was sometimes hard for his mouth to keep up. As soon as he finished describing an idea or medical technique, he'd go flying off on another tangent.

Finally, she would write the first draft and give it to him for his review. "Then we'd go over it back and forth so many times I'd lose count," said Linde. "We ended up with it much longer than it could possibly be, and so then, of course, we had to cut entire sections." This resulted in several more rounds of Atkins digging in his heels, refusing to concede, and Linde explaining why a particular passage could be removed from the manuscript without having the book suffer. The process could be arduous and frustrating, but, in the end, Linde decided that working with Atkins was definitely worth it.

* * *

Nineteen seventy-seven saw the publication of *Dr. Atkins' Super Energy Diet*, which he viewed as a vehicle for introducing his already huge fan base to the idea of a diet that was not just focused on weight loss only but on increasing patients' energy levels and improving their health overall. Atkins believed that people would gobble up *Super Energy* with the same passion with which they had devoured *Diet Revolution* back in 1972. He may have even believed that the audience for this and subsequent books would be many times the size as that for his first book and that his fan base would continue to grow exponentially, as had been the case with the number of patients in his practice.

Atkins later would admit to a great disappointment that his non-weight-loss books never sold as well as those that solely focused on peeling off the pounds.

While he still toured and appeared on top radio and television shows to promote *Super Energy*, half of the questions posed by host and audience alike concerned the *Diet Revolution* and defending himself against accusations that he was a quack.

Super Energy served to further his theory of diet and carbohydrates and insulin production he first set forth in *Diet Revolution*, but it also showed readers how they could increase their energy level by modifying the types and amounts of foods they ate. Atkins wasn't stupid, however, and he knew the only way to get them to pay attention was by assuming the only reason a reader would buy a book with the word *diet* in the title would be to lose weight. In this regard, he deftly employed a bit of sleight of hand in the book. While he spent much of the book discussing blood sugar and how certain foods can affect it, he also included individual chapters for three other diets that used the same principles, in order to placate his critics who claimed he only was concerned with the scale.

In addition to the original *Diet Revolution* plan, he also included chapters entitled "Superenergy Weight Gaining Diet," "Superenergy Weight Maintenance Diet," and "Special Situation Diet" aimed at people who were sick, people who were about to have surgery, and women who were pregnant.

Atkins put forth some truly strange advice in the book, particularly concerning people who faithfully follow the diet and still don't lose weight. (He would retract some of these suggestions later on.) One such bit of advice was the following:

"Cut your quantities substantially below the hunger point for several days. After four or five days, your hunger will be less than it was before this maneuver."

This advice was particularly perplexing because the big selling point of his diet was that you would never be hungry. Another odd suggestion was to go to Europe. "For some strange reason," he wrote, "a trip to Europe always seems to help with weight reduction." Atkins admitted he wasn't sure why it worked, theorizing that it could be the hormones infused in meat in the United States or it could even be something in the soil in Europe. "The best results seem to be achieved in Mediterranean countries: Spain, Greece, Italy, or the south of France," he noted, adding that it was also his own favorite weight-loss technique, which was no surprise since he certainly had the income to travel overseas.

Atkins also suggested that dieters who had hit a weight-loss plateau undertake what he called the "Reversal Diet," simultaneously noting that this technique sometimes backfired. "Sometimes if you switch to an all carbohydrate diet for one week, then switch back to your [induction] level diet, the weight loss starts up all over again," he wrote. The carbs he had in mind weren't the kind found in white bread and cookies but rather a strictly vegetarian diet that focused on fruit and vegetables and whole-grain breads and cereals. In later years, however, he would recant this method as widely applicable, probably because most patients weren't as restrictive with their carbohydrates as he had advised, which inevitably would result in truly frightening increases on the scale, allowing critics to point yet more fingers at his outrageous methods.

Around the time *Super Energy Diet* came out, Dr. E. Hugh Luckey, who had assumed the deanship at Cornell Medical School when Atkins was in his third year there, decided with his wife, Veronica, that the time was ripe to open a health spa in the Hamptons.

While Dr. Luckey had traveled a straightforward path from medical school to administration, ultimately becoming a distinguished professor of medicine at Cornell before retiring, his wife had led a comparably adventurous life, not all by choice.

She was born Veronica Kusmin in Russia in 1936. When the Nazis invaded the country in 1941, she managed to escape and fled to Vienna, where an elderly relative took her in and kept her safe for the duration of the war. Afterward, free to move around, she began serious study as an operatic soprano.

Veronica came to America in 1952 and soon began to pursue a

career on the stage. Young, beautiful, and supremely talented, she easily secured roles in numerous traveling productions, including a performance of *Candide* in the fall of 1958, where she played the minor role of Gretchen. A program note from the show's October 14, 1958, performance at Duke University, states, "All roles after the first five may have been performed by local talent, a common practice in touring productions," which meant that Veronica was probably living in or around eastern Pennsylvania at the time.

In 1968, she was listed as a cast member playing a Roman Doll in the movie *Dr. Coppelius*, which starred Walter Slezak. However, after spending years traveling around the country, Veronica, like most actors and musicians, realized that she would not be able to make a satisfactory living as a performer. So she set about meeting a man who would provide her with the security she had lacked so far in her life, first in Vienna, then on the road.

She met and married Dr. Hugh Luckey, who, like Robert Atkins, liked to spend time in the company of women who happened to be in show business, so it was a good match, at least in the beginning. Then, in 1977, the Luckeys bought a lavish English castle–style mansion in Bridgehampton—the less tony part of the Hamptons, the same town that Atkins himself favored—and transformed it into the island's first residential health spa at a time when spas were a relatively new concept and the popular term was *fat farm.*

There's a good chance that the spa was more Veronica's idea than her husband's. Since she was no longer performing, she needed an outlet for her creative energies. And while Dr. Luckey was pretty much retired at that point and had long looked forward to spending his free time relaxing, perhaps he went along with her wishes because he thought it would save their marriage. (The Luckeys would be divorced just five years after they opened the spa.)

The original castle was built in 1912 by John Berwind, a coal magnate who was involved in a perpetual contest to outdo his brother, who had built a luxurious mansion, known as "The Elms," in Newport, Rhode Island. Berwind christened his place "Minden" and it cost $850,000. The property had become run-down when the Luckeys purchased it from the Presbyterian Conference Association in June 1977. They paid a mere $200,000 for it.

Veronica took it upon herself to set the tone of the resort, even attending a decorating class or two to bring herself up to speed. "I spent months haunting auctions in the city and visiting showrooms to get it just right," she said. The main house contained fifteen bedrooms, while the outbuildings added another eleven. Besides updating the electrical system—the original still being in place from when the house was first built—the roof also had to be repaired, and every room in the house needed to be repainted and furnished. While the renovation was going on, Woody Allen filmed parts of his movie *Interiors* there.

Veronica had become immersed in the world of weight loss while married to Dr. Luckey in the late 1970s, and it's hard to believe that their paths hadn't crossed with Atkins's at some point during the decade. The official line was that her divorce had just become final when she met Atkins at a party in 1984. However, it's likely that in the spring of 1978, when the popularity of Atkins's low-carb diet was on the wane just as low-fat programs were beginning to appear on the horizon, and given their Cornell connection, that both Veron- ica and Hugh could have been patients of Atkins's at the time they opened their health spa. As *The New York Times* reported in a feature on Minden that appeared on March 7, 1978, the gray slacks that Dr. Luckey wore at the time of the interview were baggy, which he said was the result of losing "twenty pounds on a low-carbohydrate diet in preparation for the spa's opening."

When it came to planning the fare that would be served to guests, the Luckeys understood the current dietary trend, and chose to feature a low-fat, seven-hundred-calorie menu revolving around bean sprouts, yogurt, and fruit salad. Guests also had the option to participate in a modified fast using Optifast protein drinks. The Atkins diet was nowhere in sight.

Robert Atkins probably saw the same shift in diet popularity, but he decided to keep on plugging away in the hopes that his re- vamped message in his *Super Energy Diet* book would be heard. "I don't consider myself a selfless individual," he said. "But this frus- tration I feel at not getting my idea across to the public in general, and the medical profession in particular, has become the overriding factor in my personality."

Atkins was a single-minded individual with an agenda to push and little time left over for anything else. But, then, he really wasn't that interested in what was going on in the world at the time and he didn't much care.

"There was nothing in the conversations that I had with him that led me to believe that he was a pop culture diva," said Roger

Rapoport, adding that this personality quirk was the norm among the other high-profile physicians he had interviewed for his book. "Like a lot of people who are highly focused, he didn't necessarily read *Rolling Stone* or go to a lot of rock concerts. Plus, he had lots of people who would do things for him, run errands, that sort of thing, so he really didn't have to bother with the real world."

The surprising thing about Robert Atkins is that even with the media spotlight and attention on him—good and bad—he wasn't a snob about who he was or what he was able to accomplish. Obstinate, yes. But snobby? No.

In his profile on Atkins, Rapoport described how they stopped at a Howard Johnson's restaurant on the way back to Manhattan from their weekend in the Hamptons. Despite the fact that back in the 1970s fine-dining establishments were not found with the same abundance that they are today, the assumption is that with his fame, his money, and his love for modern art, he would rather drop dead than be seen in such a common restaurant. But unlike others raised in a lower-class setting who failed to acknowledge publicly their roots unless it served a purpose, Atkins always tended to be open about his background and where he had come from. So stopping at a Howard Johnson's made a huge impression on Rapoport even though as soon as they sat down Atkins picked up the bottle of ketchup on the table and started to deconstruct the ingredients label in terms of carbohydrate content.

And because Atkins was so focused on his medicine and so hopelessly out of it, he could also be unwittingly naïve and charming at the same time.

At this same Howard Johnson's, one of the young female roommates who hitched a ride back to the city started to tremble, which Atkins noticed.

"I bet you have low blood sugar," he said.

She asked why, and he replied, "Because many people who have it shake like you do. You should come in and let me give you a glucose tolerance test."

"I don't think that's necessary," she said. "I shake because I was on coke for several years."

"I knew it," said Atkins, "another Coca-Cola addict."

At that point, she started to laugh.

"Not Coca-Cola, cocaine!" she said.

Around this time, Atkins moved out of his one-bedroom apartment to a penthouse on Sutton Place. Compared with the showy new money of York Avenue and the old money of Park Avenue, Sutton Place was understated wealth. It was as if people who were secure with their lives lived here; they didn't need to be in the middle of everything to constantly show it off. It was quieter, calmer, despite the mad rush of the FDR/East River Drive that droned by twenty-four hours a day.

He lived in a newer building, twenty floors up, with a commanding view of the river.

The serenity of Sutton Place almost seemed a bit schizophrenic, in contrast to his life outside his apartment, since Atkins spent his waking hours at the center trying to gain acceptance for his diet every minute of every day. His choosing Sutton Place may have been a place of "forced" respite, perhaps, where he could just escape everything, even if only for overnight.

Of course, Atkins also knew that having a penthouse apartment on Sutton Place would only help his cachet with the ladies. With his extensive collection of art—stacked in office stairways at times since there was no more wall space left to hang them—he had a perfectly plausible reason for asking women if they wanted to come up to his apartment to see his etchings.

In a way, Robert Atkins's naïveté in the ways of the world still extended to his most vociferous critics, which included other doctors as well as the media. If only they'd read the literature, talked to my patients, examined my records, they'd believe, he honestly thought.

But while he kept up his public persona, Atkins began to branch out a bit. For one, he was starting to investigate alternative medical treatments—like acupuncture, chiropractic, and other, more radical techniques—to incorporate into his practice.

If he thought his foray into alternative medicine would do nothing to enhance his reputation with doctors who were entrenched in the world of traditional medicine, he was right.

The gloves were about to come off. And if Atkins realized it, well, he didn't much care.

5.

THE TWILIGHT ZONE

A s the 1980s began, low-carb was beginning to lessen in the national weight-loss consciousness, no thanks to the constant onslaught of criticism hurled at Robert Atkins since *Diet Revolution* was published. At the same time, some previously unfamiliar medical practices from China and other Far Eastern countries were beginning to appear on these shores, and since Atkins was always interested in anything that raised the ire of orthodox medicine he avidly began to investigate these alternatives. In order to do that, he had to add more physicians to his practice while continuing to build up his clientele; after all, longtime patients were beginning to defect in droves because even the government had gotten into the act, telling Americans they should eat less fat in their diets . . . *much* less.

Atkins carefully selected the physicians he wanted to work with him. Since he regarded himself as primarily a practitioner of alternative medicine, he knew he needed to balance his more radical approach toward medicine by hiring physicians who were more conventional. In the early 1980s, after all, the popular opinion of acupuncture, chiropractic, and other unorthodox treatments was that they were ineffective at best, downright dangerous at worst.

So Dr. Atkins had to tread lightly. He found many future colleagues at the medical conferences he still faithfully attended. He always was trying to further his knowledge, and, of course, he was never satisfied with what he knew.

Medical author Arline Brecher was one of Atkins's harshest critics when she was working with Dr. Neil Solomon. After she left him, she hadn't found another physician to align herself with or whose views she respected. Then she bumped into Dr. Atkins at a medical conference in the early 1980s. Like him, she was a frequent conference attendee.

The subject was chelation therapy, and Brecher, who was wandering around the exhibit hall, caught sight of Atkins out of the corner of her eye, going from booth to booth, all the while taking notes on a yellow legal pad. "Nobody was paying any attention to him, and I knew he wasn't on the program as a speaker, so I went over and asked him why he was there by himself," she said.

Atkins was kind of embarrassed, as if she had caught him doing something he shouldn't. Telling her to keep her voice down, since he obviously didn't want anyone to know he was there, he explained he was attending the conference as a student because he wanted to learn about chelation. They spoke some more, and Brecher came away from their meeting impressed with Atkins's views on alternative medicine. While they never worked together, at least they weren't the bitter enemies they had been in years past.

Atkins always looked forward to meeting professionals like himself who were disgusted with orthodox medicine, because it made him feel like he wasn't so alone in his choice to stray from the tried and true.

Atkins not only welcomed contact professionally; he also welcomed it socially. In his daily practice, it was a rare moment that Atkins could claim for himself, though he would court his nurses and patients to satisfy his romantic life. But conventions provided a social outlet that, due to his increasing fame and demands on his time, pretty much restricted him to the medical field, except for his regular one-night stands.

But even with other medical professionals, conversation never strayed far from the battle at hand. Other physicians were as caught up in their own struggles with the medical establishment as Atkins was, so they rarely spoke about their own personal lives, another trait they shared.

"We were pretty well stuck in the rut of railing against the establishment," said Warren Levin, M.D., a physician who opened New York's first holistic health center in 1974, "and not sharing the warm wrinkles of time."

Aside from scouting out future colleagues at these medical conferences, Atkins often found them among his patients who either joined his staff or became regular business colleagues. In the same way that Fran Gare was a patient of Atkins before eventually becoming his coauthor and medical director, Kurt Greenberg, author of *Challenging Orthodoxy*, in which he featured Atkins in a lengthy profile, first met him as a patient. In 1983, the muscles in Greenberg's legs had suddenly become so weak that he could hardly walk, and since he was usually very active, walking four or five miles a day, he was extremely worried. He visited a battery of medical specialists, from physicians to podiatrists to chiropractors. No one could pinpoint the cause of his trouble.

Finally, he made an appointment with Atkins, whom he considered to be a last resort. The first thing Atkins did was to give Greenberg a glucose tolerance test, a standard procedure he administered to most new patients by that time.

"It's a horrible test," said Greenberg. "I drank this heavy Coke syrup and within minutes I got the shakes and my stomach started churning." A few hours later, after all of his reactions were charted and noted by the nurses, Atkins returned and said, "You're way down on your potassium," and that was it. He prescribed some potassium supplements, and, within ten days, Greenberg was again walking five miles a day at his previous speed.

"Atkins honed in on the problem pretty quickly, which no one else was able to do," he said. Greenberg continued to see him as a patient for a few months, and then began working with Atkins in connection with a vitamin supplement company that Greenberg collaborated with, to advise him on new products, protocols, and studies. He also worked with other doctors who were learning about alternative medicine.

"They were all somewhat competitive with each other, since they all had nontraditional practices in the New York area, and there were only so many patients to go around," he said. "But they had a common cause that bound them together."

The physicians got their information wherever they could, since it wasn't likely to be written up in mainstream medical publications like *JAMA* or the *New England Journal of Medicine.* So the same group of doctors went to the same conferences and informally traded notes, and, in an eerie foreshadowing of how physicians today rely on the pharmaceutical industry to recommend medications, turned to the supplement companies for cutting-edge advice.

"They would depend on us to tell them about new products," Kurt Greenberg said.

Atkins was so heartened by networking with other medical professionals who believed the same thing that before long they decided to form an organization that would represent them, in order to present a united front against the critics. That group was FAIM, the Foundation for the Advancement of Innovative Medicine.

"They initially formed the group to support a couple of the doctors who were under attack for doing chelation therapy in the New York area, and then expanded it so that it could become influential beyond the state of New York," said Arline Brecher, who added, "there would not have been any FAIM if it had not been for Bob." Not coincidentally, once Atkins had the support of a group behind him, he proceeded to become more aggressive not only about using alternative methods in his practice but also about bragging about the results he was getting. Every chance he got, he would announce that he could cure 95 percent of disease with nutritional support and with fewer side effects than other doctors who relied on drugs. He was challenged on that statement many times.

"But he never said that he *wouldn't* use pharmaceuticals,"

Greenberg added, explaining that many of the alternative physicians he worked with through the years had solid experience using traditional pharmaceuticals, which was probably a major reason why they worked so hard to get patients off of them before replacing them with more natural therapeutics.

It wasn't long before Atkins's determination to use alternative medicine to cure illness merged with the methods he used to measure the success of his diet. And as he was rewarded by patients who saw him solely for weight loss, he was equally rewarded by those who saw him for a chronic illness. "If we take a multiple sclerosis patient who comes in in a wheelchair and that patient ends up pushing the wheelchair because he is [now] able to walk, then the amount of nutrient loss in the urine is not an important point," he said. "The important point is the clinical response. And that's what we live by."

Once Atkins had the support of like-minded physicians behind him, his dislike of mainstream medicine and the medical establishment never wavered. Everywhere he looked he saw commonalities between his approach to diet and his approach to alternative medicine. He was particularly fond of telling patients and the media that most of the teaching hospitals, medical schools, and other institutions in the country that taught nutrition received sizable endowments from international food conglomerates and cereal manufacturers. After all, he thought, if they were teaching medical students and nutritionists that white flour and refined sugar were healthy foods, how could he ever trust the institutions when they disparaged him for practicing alternative medicine?

As he learned more about treating patients with natural remedies and without relying solely on drugs, Atkins grew more comfortable introducing a growing roster of complementary medical practices to his patients. Taking supplements quickly became a vital part of treatment.

An initial visit usually would last several hours, especially if the patient was to undergo a glucose tolerance test. Eric Westman, M.D., who worked with Atkins years later to devise a study protocol for the Atkins diet, likened Atkins's practice to that of a college or university, in that a number of employees performed the tests and then presented their findings to Atkins. "There was one doctor who conducted a hands-on evaluation, and there were nurses and other staff members who administered a number of tests," said Dr. Westman. Only when all information was gathered and all questions answered would the patient see Dr. Atkins.

For Westman, who came from a university setting, the progression made sense, since in the academic world assistants do most of the work and the guy at the top does most of the analysis. For those who favored a one-on-one, hands-on approach, Atkins's methods could seem a bit impersonal if not overwhelming.

"It was the first time I had seen an operation this size," said Dr. Bernard Raxlen of what he observed in 1983. "There were at least forty people working there in an auxiliary capacity, and the patient would have to see these people first before they would ever get their audience with Atkins himself. At the end, he would interview the patient, prescribe a standard diet handout and a whole lot of vitamins, and then direct them to the supplement department. The patient would then leave with a shopping bag full of supplements."

Raxlen thought that Atkins's interactions with patients bordered on the aloof. "I sat through a number of his visits with patients, and he definitely had an aura about him," he said. "He had the name and the books, so it was almost like coming to see a celebrity, so patients tended to keep their distance. He was polite and he was attentive and a lot of the times you know he got it right.

"But as a caring physician," he added, "that just wasn't his thing. He was a kind of nutritional surgeon, slicing through everything, and he wasn't particularly interested in your life story or your woes. He wasn't interested in the whole person, he was interested in sort of doing something to you rather than relating in a healing context."

While his practice usually lost money, especially after expanding into complementary medicine and taking on additional staff, Atkins was beginning to realize the profits that could be generated selling supplements.

"He was one of the few doctors who had incorporated the supplements into his practice to the extent where he was making lots of money," said Kurt Greenberg, who noted that most doctors who tried the same approach couldn't generate the income Atkins could. And while Atkins took chances and offered some of the more cutting-edge supplements to his patients, he tended to go with those that were backed by studies, however small, which was ironic given his usual response whenever someone asked to see a study backing his own claims.

"He liked to know what was new when it came to supplements," said Greenberg, "but he always wanted the literature that would back it up. He wouldn't go with the real fads; instead he chose those nutrients that he felt would be proven one day to be as good as the comparable pharmaceuticals, but without the side effects." For instance, Atkins felt that the supplement pantathine would be as effective in reducing cholesterol levels as the prescription drug Lipitor, and he advised his patients with potential heart problems to take it regularly.

But to make sure a supplement was safe and effective, he would usually try it out on himself first. Betty Kamen, Ph.D., a nutritional expert who often had Atkins as a guest on her syndicated radio show, was amused when he admitted to playing guinea pig. Kamen had written a book on hormone replacement therapy, and a natural products company had developed a cream using herbs and progesterone—the natural form of the hormone, as opposed to progestin, the synthetic version—based on her research. Though the purpose of the cream was to help women alleviate the symptoms of menopause, Atkins discovered a particularly creative use for it and they were discussing it on her show. "He actually said that he used this herbal progesterone cream on his face because he thought it was the best wrinkle cream that he had ever seen," Kamen said. "I thought it was pretty interesting for him to come right out and say this on the air, that he was a man who was using this cream for women and [it] was helping decrease his wrinkles."

In fact, he was always trying out the newest alternative medical techniques that he would read about in journals or that sales reps from supplement companies would show to him. He sucked on candies made from colloidal silver, considered to be a natural form of antibiotic, and participated in an iridology session, where studying the eye is supposed to reveal the health of the body. So strongly did he believe in the use of supplements, Atkins also took more than fifty of his own vitamin and mineral formulations every day, and he even opted to use ozone instead of chlorine to keep the pool in his Hamptons house clean and free of bacteria.

To Atkins, experimentation was nothing new, and nothing to be embarrassed about. "Throughout the history of mankind, the effectiveness of a doctor in treating a patient depended on a relationship between the healer and the *healee*," he said. "And, for the healer to be effective, he has got to believe that he is a healer. He really, in essence, has got to believe that whatever he's got in there works."

Dr. Atkins had learned so much since entering the world of alternative medicine that he felt that he was ready to tell the world at large between the covers of yet another diet book. In 1981, *Dr. Atkins' Nutrition Breakthrough*, his third book, was published. Though it generated significant attention—the angle taken by more pessimistic media outlets was, "Here he goes again"—it didn't come close to matching the sales figures generated by *Diet Revolution*, just as *Super Energy* hadn't.

But Atkins wasn't upset, unlike with the second book. At this point he was so excited about unorthodox medical practices that he decided to officially christen his practice "The Atkins Center for Complementary Medicine" in 1984. The center would also serve to distance himself from low carbs in the public's eye, all but forgotten anyway in the then current aerobicized low-fat movement. From the beginning, Atkins had intended the center to rival the Mayo

Clinic, albeit for alternative medicine, envisioning departments headed up by the leading experts in given fields, from acupuncture to chiropractic.

From the time that Robert Atkins first became a celebrity doctor in the early 1970s, people were always contacting him with new ideas about how to expand his practice or capitalize on his name. He usually would hear them out, inviting them to outline their ideas, sometimes asking them to come into the office to talk.

"He always felt that his practice was going to be prestigious someday, and because of that he thought he should offer other alternatives to medications other than the diets," said Bernard Raxlen. "And he knew he couldn't do it all himself, and so he welcomed hearing from others. He was always looking for entrepreneurial and creative ways to expand the opportunities for his theories and methodologies. You know, he had essentially given birth to the child that was his practice and his career, and since he didn't have children I always thought that he looked on his business as his baby." So while Atkins was eager to help shape the practice's future, he could also be very proprietary about handing over any part of it to somebody else. In addition, he had a tendency to change his mind once a deal was closed.

By 1983, Dr. Raxlen had developed a thriving practice in complementary medicine in Connecticut, but he wanted to move to Toronto to launch a practice there. He was thinking about selling his Connecticut practice to a like-minded physician, and he knew about Atkins and his refocused approach to medicine, so Raxlen contacted him to see if he was interested in operating a satellite office in

Connecticut. After all, not everyone wanted to head into the city every time she had a doctor's appointment if she could help it.

Raxlen had called Atkins on a lark, and he was surprised when Atkins said he wanted to pursue the idea. Acquiring another physician's practice, especially in another state, was not something many doctors would do. As negotiations proceeded, the two agreed that Raxlen would run the office for another year, as a consultant, after Atkins bought it, and in the meantime Atkins would train another doctor to take it over then, so Raxlen could move to Toronto.

The terms were agreed upon, a contract was signed, and Raxlen got to work setting up labs in Atkins's New York office and training Atkins's staff, since Raxlen had been practicing alternative medicine for many more years than Atkins. It didn't take long for Raxlen to see that the center actually resembled a typical dysfunctional family unit.

"He had this vision from the beginning of the center as a holistic supermarket where people could get treated by a bona fide celebrity doctor," said Raxlen. While the majority of patients stayed with Atkins for years, there were some who became pretty disgruntled.

"They wanted Bob Atkins," he said, "that's what attracted them to the Atkins Center. But most of the time, they didn't get Bob Atkins for more than a few minutes in the course of an appointment that could easily last a couple of hours between medical testing and workups and waiting for lab results.

"It was like he was the ringleader and he operated the practice within the confines of his circus tent," he said. "Before he even saw a patient for the first time, Atkins would already have all the patient's data on his desk so when it came for the audience with the

King, Atkins only needed a few minutes to review the lab results and map out a plan." While this was a very efficient way to run a large medical practice, some patients felt like the process was fragmented, and they were falling through the cracks.

But even if a patient did manage to spend more than a few minutes with Dr. Atkins, he or she might not have liked it. Dr. Raxlen's wife, Maryann, worked for a time at Atkins's clinic, helping to train the staff and manage front office operations.

"I'd spend the day in the office and he just wasn't there for his patients," she said. "They never got the eye contact, they never got the half hour, they never got to know his hand on their heart. If they were lucky, they got a few minutes with him, and that was it. Somewhere along the way, the center turned into a huge factory of medicine."

According to Maryann, the assembly-line quality at the center also affected the staff. "They were some of the most unreliable people I had ever worked with," she said. But, at the same time, she couldn't entirely blame the employees.

"You know how the tone has to be set at the top of any organization, but that wasn't the case at the center," she said, adding that the staff wasn't sure what to do with these really sick patients and a doctor who spent only a few minutes with each one, not to mention the rope 'em in, herd 'em out process at the center. "They were like lost sheep," she said. In fact, she says that employees used to call her "The Shepherdess."

It was soon apparent to Robert Atkins and Bernard Raxlen that it was a bad match, with different expectations on both sides. While both parties were outspoken promoters of complementary medicine, one believed in spending at least thirty minutes with each patient who walked in the door, the other five minutes at most.

The high-traffic patient model Atkins had developed was yet another example of his inability to say that no matter how much he had more would always be better. Part of his motivation for the ever-increasing patient load perhaps was because he may have wanted to say to his critics, "The twenty-five thousand patients I've treated over the years can't be wrong," or he may have wanted to just thumb his nose at practitioners of orthodox medicine. In fact, patient validation eventually would become more important to him than validation from the medical establishment. And, of course with Atkins, it's always the more the merrier.

Raxlen admits that the conflict could have been avoided by admitting early on the differences between themselves when it came to patient load. And then when Raxlen reiterated that he didn't want to move to Manhattan, it didn't take long for Atkins to start nudging Raxlen to alter the terms of the contract after it had been signed.

"He really wanted to transfer the entire business to New York where he could incorporate it into his practice, but I told him there were lots of patients who wouldn't travel to New York to see him, and of course he didn't believe that," said Bernard Raxlen. "Then he tried to get me to move to New York and work in his practice. He said he would set me up in an apartment in Manhattan and that he wanted me to work with him, but he didn't say, 'I want you to be my business partner.'" If he had, Raxlen says, he might have considered it.

But when it became clear that Raxlen had every intention of moving to Canada, and Atkins didn't get his way, things quickly began to deteriorate. As Atkins had learned from his father, when something didn't work out the way he had anticipated he tried to cut his losses and a new deal at the same time.

Atkins told Raxlen he wanted to back out of the deal, and that he wanted the $130,000 back that he had already paid toward the purchase of the practice.

Raxlen refused, and Atkins filed a lawsuit against him, alleging that Raxlen had falsely represented the income the Connecticut practice was generating and that zoning restrictions in Ridgefield, where the practice was located, precluded office expansion or the addition of more employees. A third point of contention revolved around whether Raxlen could legally consult in New York since his medical license was issued in Connecticut.

Raxlen was surprised when he was served with papers: Atkins was suing him for the return of $130,000, in addition to punitive damages. It is evident from testimony given at the 1987 trial that Atkins relied on the same emotional intuitiveness and lack of proof that motivated his own practice. He knew what he has seen and experienced, so why bother with documentation and witnesses?

One intriguing moment arose at the trial when Raxlen's lawyer, John J. Reilly, asked Atkins, "Do you think Dr. Raxlen was fraudulent?"

Atkins replied, "No, I never said he was fraudulent."

"But it says right here that you are suing him for fraud," said Reilly.

"Well, that is just in a manner of speaking," said Atkins, offering no further explanation.

The balance of the trial concerned minutiae about the contract and what constituted "net receipts" and disputes over who was responsible for certain bills, from lab tests to uniforms to postage and laundry expenses for the lab Raxlen had set up at the center.

The verdict, issued in 1988, found that Robert Atkins was in breach of contract. They never spoke to each other again.

Dr. Atkins recovered from the setback. After all, there were always other physicians eager to work at the center, and there were always other people with ideas who would beg him to put his name on their venture, ranging from health spas to franchised Atkins Centers in every major city of the country. Some new, elaborate scheme that its sponsor promised would be the crowning glory of Atkins's practice seemed to come along at least once a week.

And he lent most of them his ear. But 99 percent of them never even got as far as Bernard Raxlen, in part because Atkins wanted either a ridiculous amount of money or the majority share in the business, or he asked for something so outrageous that the deal would never proceed past the initial meeting. But as Len Lipson, who worked at the center for eleven years, described it, money had nothing to do with his extreme demands.

"It was as if he gave everything he had for so many years, and sacrificed so much that he felt that he was entitled to get something back to reimburse him for the grief and criticism he had endured," said Lipson. And maybe it went deeper: in the face of all this negativity, there were people who wanted to work with him anyway, who clearly valued his name. He was flattered by the courtship ritual, which is why he was always willing to listen.

But these people didn't value the Atkins diet as much as he did, since they hadn't lived through it, so he'd toss out some ridiculous deal or another that would end the conversation with most of them. And in the unlikely event that they agreed to his terms, he would do something to muck it up or anger the other party so that the deal never saw the light of day.

"Some people had the mistaken impression that he was a very money-grubbing kind of guy," said Len Lipson. "Really, he had no objection to making money, but that wasn't what really drove him."

Another reason why business deals rarely went anywhere with Atkins had to do with the way the practice was run, the dysfunctional-family aspect.

"It was difficult for him to truly give somebody else the credit for stuff because he lived a life in which nobody gave him any credit at all," said Lipson. "It felt like no matter what we tried to do, we just couldn't get out of our own way," he added, noting that Atkins exacerbated the problem by trying to micromanage his staff.

As a result, Atkins needed to know everything that was going on at the practice down to the smallest details, which resulted in a high staff turnover and therefore more of a sense of disorganization. He could also be extremely impatient. It's almost as if he suffered from a peculiar form of ADD (Attention Deficit Disorder), wherein a person starts a business, runs it for a while, then finds starting a business better than running one and so they sell it and start another.

In other words, Robert Atkins was a serial entrepreneur in a physician's body.

"At the end of the day, he wanted to know where the balance sheet stood and how much money had been billed that day," said Maryann Raxlen. "Perhaps this was because he grew up in an entrepreneurial family where every penny counted, or he lived in a world where his contributions were not valued by the majority. But by keeping track of the balance sheet, at least he could feel somewhat validated despite the fact that his practice consistently lost money."

"I don't know how to make a profit," he once said.

When Atkins later sold supplements, and then shakes and energy bars, it was clear he viewed these commercial offshoots as nothing more than a part-time hobby.

Over the course of the 1980s, Dr. Atkins continued to plug away at his practice, learning new therapies, attending conferences and seminars, and generally heaping more on his plate. And just when staff and colleagues warned him not to get involved in one more activity or else they'd have to clone him, Atkins took on an assignment that for anyone else would have been the equivalent of two full-time jobs even with help.

He began to host a nightly radio show on WOR in New York called *Design for Living*, which he took over from Carlton Fredericks, a man considered by industry insiders to be the father of alternative medicine and nutritional healing. Indeed, Atkins considered him one of his mentors.

Starting in the 1940s, Fredericks was an early proponent of using nutrition to cure disease. He zeroed in on hypoglycemia particularly and how refined sugar and white flour stressed the body, which is how Atkins first discovered him. Unlike Atkins, Fredericks was not a medical doctor but a self-trained nutritionist. His doctorate was a Ph.D. in communications. He initially came on the scene talking about diet before branching out into complementary medicine. Like Atkins, he quickly developed a reputation as a quack or worse, discredited by traditional medical practitioners and the AMA.

Nonetheless, Fredericks was a prolific media spokesman, appearing frequently on radio and television shows and in newspaper and magazine articles and columns, including, among others, *Prevention Magazine.* In 1976, he began hosting a nightly radio show on nutrition and natural health syndicated around the country, and his reputation spread.

Carlton Fredericks and Robert Atkins first met after *Diet Revolution* was published, and they kept in close contact over the years, trading notes and informing each other about new alternative practices. In the 1980s, Fredericks served as a freelance consultant at the Atkins Center, conducting individual sessions with patients. Atkins, in turn, made frequent appearances on his radio show.

When Fredericks died in 1987, at the age of seventy-seven, producers and executives alike felt that the show should continue and that the most likely replacement for Fredericks was Atkins, although they did interview several other candidates, including Dr. Warren Levin.

"I thought about it, but I chickened out," Levin said, blaming the schedule more than anything else, which consisted of one hour nightly Monday through Friday, beginning at ten o'clock eastern time, with the occasional Saturday thrown in as well. "I honestly didn't know anyone who could handle it." Of course, that's when Robert Atkins said he'd do it. He changed the name of the show to *Your Health Choices*, and it ran until he died.

"I think he did an incredible job with that show," said Levin. "He would be in the office at seven-thirty in the morning and go all out until the show ended just before eleven. With his schedule, I honestly don't know how he had time to go to the bathroom, let alone host a nightly radio show. I did a weekly Saturday morning radio show for a year and a half, and it was a real drag," he adds.

And still, even with his breakneck schedule, Atkins continued to expand his practice, write books, albeit with the help of ghost-writers, add to his art collection, and date as many women as he could juggle. Unlike the image he regularly presented to his critics and the media, the image he had of himself was that of an old softy. "I'm a pussycat," he said. "[I'm] one of these Libras who see both sides of everything and tend to be forgiving."

The people who really knew him, of course, saw right through him. "He always goes for the shock value," Colette Heimowitz, who worked as director of nutrition at the center, said.

The truth was that like many people who have achieved a lot in their lives, Atkins was so certain about his ideas that he didn't want to compromise. "There wasn't much give in him," said Kurt Greenberg. "I think that he pushed himself a little too hard, for sure. Going up against the establishment as he did was incredibly stressful for him, and he faced it on a daily basis. On the other hand, if he hadn't pursued promoting a low-carb diet, he would have made his mark elsewhere."

Eric Westman, who would work with him later, agreed. "I remember him pounding his fist on the table during his radio show because he thought so strongly about something and he was very emphatic about his point," he said. "But the guy would have been very devoted to whatever he was doing."

Dr. Atkins' Health Revolution was published in 1988, and it focused solely on complementary medicine, not only in an attempt to change the way that traditional medicine operated by motivating the patients themselves to participate but also to encourage people who bought his diet books to become as interested in alternative medicine as they were in a low-carb diet.

"Suppose *Health Revolution* is as successful as *Diet Revolution*," Atkins said. "Suppose that it is read by ten million people. If that were the case, there wouldn't be ten million people trying to figure out how to lose twelve pounds, there would be ten million people pondering, philosophically, over questions of what is medicine, what is science, what is healing?"

Unfortunately, Atkins non-diet books sold only a fraction of what his low-carb books sold. Though he was always dismayed that they didn't reach a larger audience, he never stopped trying to get the word out. In fact, he often said that the only thing that would win people over to complementary medicine was if he could cure a disease that orthodox medicine hadn't been able to cure. "This revolution needs the cure of an incurable illness," he asserted.

Even though Atkins considered his colleagues in the alternative medicine field as friends and colleagues, he undoubtedly ruffled more than a few feathers by frequently proclaiming himself the prime mover behind the industry.

"If I am the leader of the movement, this is one leader who knows the political side of it," he said. "Battle scars are political. I believe this is my role in life, to be the battle-scarred veteran who leads this public relations war against the establishment."

Despite the fact that he could handle a workload that was more than enough for ten people, the one aspect of his more-is-better life that he actually began to tire of was the social. Though Atkins still regularly described himself as "a very active bachelor," he later admitted that his lengthy bachelorhood "was not an accomplishment. I would meet people at parties who were beautiful, but the quality wasn't there."

Until he ran into Veronica Luckey, that is.

From the beginning, Veronica was different from the young models and actresses he tended to favor. She was attractive and thin, yes, but she was in a totally different league. For one thing, as the ex-wife of the retired dean of Cornell Medical School Veronica had already breathed the rarified air of the Upper East Side for several decades.

Plus, she had European style. She was classy and brainy—she spoke eight languages—and, like Atkins, she hailed from a Russian Jewish background. In other words, he was instantly comfortable with her since they had so much in common.

Veronica was also a strong woman in her own right, and, unlike most of the other women in his life, she made demands on him that the others never would have since they viewed him more as an icon and avenue to riches than as an equal, as she did. After all, she had her own money from her divorce settlement so she didn't need his, though, admittedly, his wealth was many times hers.

Perhaps the most important point is that of all the women who spent time with Robert Atkins, Veronica was the first to remind him of another classy, strong woman who he greatly respected: Norma, his mother.

"Veronica was Bob's definition of self," said Maryann Raxlen. "She completed him, in that sense, so I think they were a really good match."

She also stood by him and defended him to anyone who dared to utter a harsh word. "Though he never admitted it, he always had a lot of trouble personally dealing with his critics," said a former colleague. "Veronica had a thicker skin than he did, which I think was due to her European background, so she had a different view of criticism and could handle it better."

After decades of struggle, Robert Atkins felt like he was entitled to some type of reward for his hard work. Perhaps Veronica Luckey was the first person in his life who totally validated him, and he trusted her implicitly. While other girlfriends may have done the same thing, she was different. More important, while the other women he had dated would have tolerated his cheating because they thought he might eventually come back, Veronica made it clear from the beginning that she would not put up with any philandering.

At the age of fifty-six, maybe Atkins had finally realized how ridiculous it was for a man his age to chase after women half as young.

Or maybe he was just tired of the chase itself and was ready to settle down.

The two married in 1988, in a ceremony out in the Hamptons, and colleagues say that marriage immediately changed him, calming him down. "She certainly gave him another focus," said Warren Levin. "He seemed very happy to give up his former status as one of New York City's most eligible bachelors."

Though the low-fat craze had been around since the early 1980s, and had already put a significant dent in Dr. Atkins's empire, the absolute death knell came in 1988 when the surgeon general presented the results of a detailed study of nutrition in a 712-page report. Though few nutrition experts or representatives of the media read the entire tome, all they had to hear was one simple piece of advice: Cut down on all fats in the diet while increasing fiber.

As a result, patients fled Atkins's practice in droves, even if they were not seeing him for dietary reasons, and staffers began to wonder why they were sticking with such an obvious loser. Plus, Atkins's reputation solidified in media circles as someone to fill the "quack" seat on a panel discussion but nothing more.

The writing was on the wall: Low-fat, though already a pronounced trend in the food industry, was about to explode in the American diet, sending low-carb sausage-and-egg breakfasts to history's dustbin. As a result, Dr. Atkins decided to pursue his passion, complementary medicine, more aggressively. Having already won his other first true love—Veronica—perhaps he felt comfortable with striking off in another, equally controversial direction that he didn't entirely agree with. In the wake of the low-fat craze and increased scrutiny on his alternative practices, somebody needed to toss Atkins a life preserver. And none of the business plan-of-the-week people who came through his door would do it for him, either.

For help, he would turn to his patients.

6.

A PACT WITH THE DEVIL

As the end of the 1980s came upon him, Dr. Atkins continued to promote his low-carb diet, always refusing to cede any ground to those who lambasted his ideas as unhealthy and who called him a quack. TV and radio talk show producers only booked him when they needed a foil for the lead-off guest, inevitably one of the leading low-fat diet experts of the day. Despite his media status as second-class diet doctor, Atkins seemed unfazed by it all.

However, the constant attacks continued to exact their toll on his patient load. It was becoming increasingly difficult to attract new patients—and to keep old ones—when it seemed like the whole world was moving in lockstep against him. One by one, they began to look to other physicians. Staff members recall the constant exodus of medical records as extremely disheartening.

The patients who stayed, however, were extremely loyal to both Atkins and his low-carb diet. But they had one major complaint: In a fast-paced world where everything was low in fat or high in carbohydrates, or both, it was difficult to find something that they could eat on the run while still remaining on the low-carb program. They had no time to prepare their own snacks. Perhaps something like the low-fat energy bars sold in convenience stores would be great, only low-carb instead.

Atkins hesitated, and for good reason. One of the things he constantly stressed with his patients was that they should eat foods that were as close to their natural state as possible, and, for him, any kind of energy bar was as good as poison since it was clearly a processed food.

There was another reason for his reluctance. "He was always very careful of the value of his name, and that's why he never wanted to franchise his name out while he was alive," said Fred Pescatore, who worked as Atkins's medical director in the 1990s.

But his patients continued to beg him for something—"You sell the vitamins and other supplements, why not energy bars?" they reasoned—and so, with great reluctance, he gave in and developed not only an energy bar but also a low-carb shake that would make it easier for patients to keep to their Atkins programs.

"As long as you only use it for emergencies," he reminded them.

While Atkins was at it, he figured he might as well include a list of the dietary supplements he sold to his patients in New York. He named the offshoot "Complementary Formulations," and put together a list of products and prices so that dieters all over the country could order supplements through the mail, since no store at the time would think of stocking them. Despite its simple design in a world of slickly produced, four-color catalogs that resembled magazines, the orders began streaming in from the very first mailing.

On a late spring day in 1991, Stuart Fischer, M.D., the medical director at the Atkins Center, finally felt that his partner was relying too much or alternative medical treatments.

For several weeks, Atkins had had conjunctivitis in his right eye and it had gotten progressively worse. When the condition first developed, most patients weren't aware of it since his primary contact with patients was him sitting behind that mammoth desk in his private office.

So for a while, it was easy for Atkins to conceal his condition from patients. But for those who were there for the first time, or who required his alternative medicine expertise and therefore a close physical examination by him, it was getting more difficult to hide. In fact, some patients had asked the nursing staff about it on their way out of the office. The nurses, in turn, passed along the comments to Fischer, who was the only one there capable of confronting Atkins; the majority of staffers either were too intimidated or they felt it wasn't their place to dispense medical advice to Atkins.

Fischer had mentioned the condition to Atkins several times since it first flared up, but Atkins always brushed him off. Finally, Fischer cornered him near the nurse's station.

"It will clear up by itself," said Atkins.

"But you're at risk of infecting the patients and staff. Let me at least give you some antibiotic eye drops," Fischer said, offering to administer the medication himself.

"I said it will clear up by itself," Atkins repeated, his voice tight.

"Bob, what are you so afraid of?"

"Traditional medicine is for traditional doctors," he barked. "It has nothing to offer me." He pushed past Fischer, and headed for his office.

A few days later, Atkins's eye had turned a bright shade of cherry red. It was glaringly apparent even from across the room, let alone across his desk. Fischer decided to take matters into his own hands. After the last patient had gone for the day, he grabbed a bottle of prescription eye drops from the locked medicine cabinet, knocked on Atkins's door, and let himself in.

Atkins looked up from his desk, saw the bottle in Fischer's hand, and immediately stood up, bracing his hands against the desk.

"No, Stu."

"Patients are starting to talk, Bob," said Fischer.

"They are?" Atkins looked surprised, then resumed his combative stance. "Then why haven't they said anything about it to me?"

Then he smiled at Fischer and relaxed slightly, as he realized how ridiculous that sounded.

Fischer twisted the cap off the bottle as he approached the desk. Atkins didn't move. At over six feet tall, he towered over his colleague. But Fischer wasn't deterred.

"Come on, Bob, it's not going to go away by itself."

"I've been working on it, chamomile compresses, zinc tablets, beta-carotene—"

"But they're not working," countered Fischer. "It has to be a bacterial infection, and you know that means one thing." He waved the bottle.

Atkins frowned. "But that's traditional medicine."

"Sometimes traditional is the only thing that works."

Atkins sat down heavily and slumped back in his chair with a sigh. Fischer thought it unnerving to see him in such a submissive position, for sometimes even he, who worked so closely with Atkins day in and day out, found it hard to believe that the various faces Atkins wore for different people weren't really all an act.

Fischer leaned over Atkins, and, stretching the eyelid, saw an angry red-colored eye looking back at him. He held the bottle aloft nonetheless.

"You'll let me do this twice a day, because I know you won't do it yourself," said Fischer as he gently squeezed the bottle to apply a few drops.

Atkins nodded almost imperceptibly as he blinked a few times. "Just make sure no one finds out about this," he said quietly.

That was Robert Atkins in a nutshell. He was so concerned about the image he presented on every stage he stepped onto— with patients, with colleagues, with the media—that it was obvious he would always weigh how his slightest action might be perceived by all three and then adjust it accordingly. Atkins did this because he didn't want to be known merely as a "diet doctor." For him, the diet was not just a vehicle for conveying his broader notions about alternative medicine. For him, the two were intricately tied together.

But when it came to new physicians, while anyone working with Atkins obviously had to tow the low-carb party line and go along with his views on alternative medicine, they couldn't be as gung ho as he—after all, there could only be one star—and their backgrounds and general philosophies had to be well rooted in conventional medical practices.

There was a very good reason for this: Dr. Atkins needed a front, an M.D. who had attended medical school and was exposed to all the occupational trials and tribulations during subsequent internship and residency, just as he had endured his years at Cornell Medical School. However, that same candidate also needed to espouse a subversive attitude toward medicine in general, so that it was clear he or she was on the same page as Atkins when it came to the more unorthodox techniques he experimented with in his practice. After all, he was pretty radical for the times, even among alternative practitioners.

In 1991, Atkins had read about a new technique that was being employed in Europe called "ozone gas therapy." Two years later, he used it to treat a seventy-seven-year-old woman's breast cancer, and she suffered such side effects as numbness, blurry vision, and dizziness. Her relatives filed a complaint with the New York State medical board, and, as a result, his license was suspended.

A week later, State Supreme Court Justice Edward Greenfield ruled that Atkins's license be reinstated on condition that he no longer use ozone gas therapy. The irony is that the woman recovered and returned to Atkins as her primary physician.

Of course, this experience did nothing to endear him to orthodox practitioners, nor he to them, but it did make him more careful about the patients who did walk through the door.

From the first years of his practice, in between berating patients for not sticking to their diets, Atkins also accepted many terminally ill patients into his clinic. Among them were people suffering from cancer, diseases of the immune system, and other illnesses with particularly poor prognoses. Treatments included intravenous injections of ozone and heated anal probes for cancer patients, among other risky and unproven methods, and several lawsuits were filed by the New York State Board of Medical Examiners as well on behalf of the patients' families. Although he would be in all cases totally exonerated of all blame, the legal entanglements changed him. He decided it was time to reconsider his strategy. Atkins decided he needed other physicians on staff who would essentially serve as his cover when the authorities next came calling. They would be put in charge of treatment methods endorsed by medical boards and journals alike. Only if traditional medicine failed to help would Atkins's alternative methods be turned to, and, more often than not, they brought some degree of relief to the patient. Taking this approach, he could avoid running into trouble with medical regulators in the future.

"People are told they need surgery, and it's my job to reverse the illness without requiring surgery," he said. "If more people practiced this way, the cost of medicine would drop by 30 percent. I see high-tech, expensive intervention being behind most of the problems health care has inherited."

Atkins absolutely detested that he was forced to practice medicine in this way, that he had to waste a patient's often limited time on methods he felt certain would be ineffective. But the fact that he could hand it to a traditionally trained, board-certified, one-hundred-percent-proof medical doctor helped him alleviate his sour feelings. At least he didn't have to practice the traditional medicine himself. Atkins realized from the beginning that his unorthodoxy only served to put him in the crosshairs of state and federal authorities permanently. If the unwelcome attention, however, brought him more truly sick patients who had already tried everything and whose next stop would be hospice care, then, he decided, he would continue to practice this way.

Another major reason Atkins searched for physicians who practiced conventional medicine but were open to alternatives was the reluctance of insurance companies to reimburse patients for medical procedures performed at his office. Since his first book was published in 1972 and he began to carefully cultivate his reputation as a medical renegade, most insurance companies considered him a practitioner of alternative medicine, and it was recorded that way in a national database of physicians. Back then, once a doctor was tagged "alternative," even in the most benign way, even though he or she may have employed unorthodox treatments for less than one percent of patients— it was sufficient grounds for most insurance companies to refuse to pay any and all claims for services that were rendered in the doctor's office. This is the primary reason that when Atkins needed to fill a vacancy on his staff, he looked for doctors who were sympathetic to alternative treatments but who had strong reputations as practitioners of traditional medicine. This arrangement would not only help add balance to his practice and his reputation but would allow patients to see a "conventional" physician in the same office. The strategy assured that insurance companies would pay claims.

Doctors who worked for Atkins in this capacity said that the arrangement afforded them a degree of autonomy that they couldn't have achieved in a traditional medical practice. Fred Pescatore says that over the five years he worked as associate medical director at the center, it almost felt like he was running his own practice. "Even though it was my first job out of resident training, Atkins basically let me run my own show," he said. "Even though we all had a pretty heavy patient load, he always made time for me whenever I had questions or just wanted to talk about what was going on with my patients."

The curious thing is that even though Atkins carefully handpicked each doctor he wanted to work in his practice, the doctors themselves say they don't know why he zeroed in on them. Murray Susser, M.D., who worked as Atkins's medical director for more than a decade, says they used to run into each other at medical conventions. Pescatore, on the other hand, was picked by Atkins fresh out of medical school.

However Atkins found them initially, he asked a single question to decide whether a doctor would fit into his practice. He'd toss it off casually, during a drive on the Long Island Expressway to his country house, for instance, or over dinner with other staffers at his Sutton Place penthouse, or at a cocktail party at an alternative medical convention:

"When did you first realize that traditional medicine didn't work?"

The question also summed up succinctly the bitter attitude he held toward the traditional medical community. Atkins was no dummy; he knew how to seduce physicians into working for him by making them feel special, as though he was courting them and would consider no one else for the position.

Atkins liked to ask the question in a way that sounded like it was the first time it had occurred to him to ask it. The respondent, therefore, probably thought he or she was the only soul in the world whom Atkins had ever asked the question. Either way, it worked. The candidate's answer, and where the conversation went from there, revealed volumes to Atkins.

Candidates' answers ranged from "the first day of medical school" to "the first day of residency." One suspects that if a candidate disagreed with the premise of Atkins's question, Atkins brought the interview quickly to a close. But, regardless of the answer, Atkins would typically flatter the individual by admitting it took him months, even years, to come to that realization, and good for you. The communal laugh that followed was usually the sign that the recruit would be coming on board.

Atkins filled all of his physician vacancies in this manner. He only wished that the medical establishment and regulatory authorities would let him do it his way first without having to jump through all those damned hoops.

Robert Atkins settled into married life with Veronica, and, for the first time, everyone said that he seemed like he was at peace with himself, not so quick to pick a fight or fly off the handle at one of his critics.

Even though he was not as popular in the early 1990s as he once was, he still made the rounds of the talk-show circuit, appearing on everything from the *Today Show* to some small station in the hinterlands of the Midwest. One colleague joked that Atkins would show up at the opening of an envelope.

Fred Pescatore can certainly attest to that. While he was working at the Atkins Center, he had written a book, *Feed Your Kids Well*, which happened to be published at the same time that *Dr. Atkins' Vita-Nutrient Solution* came out, so they often appeared at book signings together all over the New York metropolitan area.

Once, after putting in a full day at the practice, and without stopping to eat first, they headed to a bookstore in Hartford, Connecticut, a good two-and-a-half-hour drive from Manhattan. Pescatore thought it was a total waste of time and didn't hesitate to tell Atkins how he felt.

"I said, Bob, how could you do this? But he told me it doesn't matter how small your audience is, you've got to get your message out," said Pescatore. "And if it means driving five hours round trip so the twenty people who show up will tell their friends, then it's as important as the *Today Show*."

No matter what kind of show Atkins appeared on, the host would inevitably introduce him as the controversial or unconventional diet doctor who let you eat all the steak and cheeseburgers you wanted; in other words, it was a more polite way to say he was a "quack." In the early days, astute viewers would see Atkins's face twitch slightly when introduced that way, but by the time the '90s rolled around he had relaxed—thanks in part to having Veronica in his life—and on subsequent TV appearances he would reveal no sign of his knee-jerk revulsion at being referred to as a lowly diet doctor.

Atkins also bucked the cosmetic surgery trend that was clearly becoming popular with other celebrity doctors at the time, but, at the same time, a makeup artist was never more than a few feet away.

In the videos Atkins made later on, he didn't seem like much of a maverick. Instead, he almost seemed slightly drunk. He looked uncomfortable in front of the camera, and though quick glimpses of his real self poked through here and there—mostly when he cracked a joke—it's as if the producers told him to act naturally, albeit in an aw-shucks, paternalistic kind of way.

The other times his personality flashed through were when he criticized the medical establishment. He seemed bored at times reading off the teleprompter. With lightly hooded eyes, trying hard to stay awake, he'd be okay if he was explaining all this stuff to a real live patient, but telling it to a camera, and without the safety of being behind his behemoth office desk, he was a fish out of water.

However, on TV shows, when he had another person to interact with, he was a different animal. He even trained himself to smile broadly whenever he heard the word *quack* instead of wincing, despite those times when a combative teleprompter reader in some third-rate Nielsen market began the interview by playing the devil's advocate.

"So you don't really believe that your diet is good for people, do you?"

Atkins was ready. He tapped his understanding of biofeedback and meditation to relax his shoulders, slow his breathing, and present a big grin to the host and camera as he explained the science behind his theories in much the same tone a father would tell a fairy tale to a three-year-old.

Most of the time, however, the patter between opening and closing credits ran toward innocent, occasionally titillating fodder for bored housewives. Members of the studio audience would *ooh* and *aah* when Atkins regaled them with tales of that morning's breakfast of eggs fried in butter, sausage and bacon—"and heavy cream in my coffee," he'd toss off for added effect. While most viewers remained unconvinced, the six-minute segments were harmless enough. And they moved a lot of books.

Then came *Geraldo*.

Coauthor Fran Gare recalls the first time the doctor invited her to appear with him on Geraldo Rivera's show in the early 1990s. "The first ten minutes went smoothly enough," she said, "but remember, this was Geraldo, who sometimes made Jerry Springer look like a nice guy." After the first commercial break, all hell broke loose when Geraldo went into the audience for questions.

Things started off heatedly when the first person to take the microphone, a woman, looked right at Atkins as she screamed, "You killed my mother!"

"I was absolutely mortified," says Gare, "all I wanted to do was to crawl off the stage. I looked over at Bob and he was about the calmest I'd ever seen him. He asked the woman for her mother's name, and he immediately recalled the medical conditions that were present, and proceeded to describe the woman's health problems, the ways in which he recommended that she improve her health as well as the ailments he told her that no medical professional would be able to help," she said. Geraldo turned to other audience members, who stood up to accuse Atkins of malpractice several more times during the show but, by the end of the show, the atmosphere had lost a lot of its tension. Indeed, the audience gave him a standing ovation at the end of the show.

Not only did Veronica clearly have a calming effect on her new husband but on his business as well, she gradually began to involve herself in the day-to-day running of the practice.

"Veronica was the brains of the supplement and food business," said Fran Gare. Shortly after they married, Veronica began to learn about the company and its inner workings. From the very beginning of their relationship, she made it clear that she wanted her husband to cut back on his workload, and so she probably believed if she got his medical practice and business endeavors better organized he would feel comfortable working fewer hours. Of course it backfired, and he subsequently discovered he could work even *more* with the increase in efficiency and productivity, and so Veronica stayed on to see what else needed work, not so much on the practice end but in the tiny supplement and food side of the business. Admittedly, when the nation was still fully caught in the mind-set of low-fat everything, there wasn't much for her to do. But once the first early signs surfaced that low-carb might be making a comeback—it began to stir in 1992 with the publication of *Dr. Atkins' New Diet Revolution*, an updated version of his first book—she got to work and soon had her hands full.

It didn't take long for her to realize that there was a lot of selling potential lying dormant in the vitamins and energy bars. To her husband, while the vitamins and supplements were vital to both the health of his patients as well as his practice—more than one colleague mentioned that the practice would be a continual money loser if it were not for the supplements—the energy bars and shakes were a necessary evil, there only because he thought his patients were too lazy to prepare the real kind of unprocessed foods that were the mainstay of his diet.

Veronica began to accompany Atkins to work each morning so she could learn all about the business and figure out how to best develop it. "She floated in and out of practice rooms, and she was very much a part of any meeting she wanted to be a part of," recalls Len Lipson, who was at the center when Veronica started to show up regularly.

"We had several conversations about how to define her role at the center, because her great advantage was that she had great influence when it came to Atkins," he said. "We could get through to him on some issues, but there were others that wouldn't get anywhere if we didn't go through her first. So we really wanted her around."

For example, while Atkins's sometimes belligerent style won him many meek and mild patients in the 1970s who didn't dare talk back to him, in the gentler and kinder '90s many more patients would walk out after the first session and never look back.

"Some patients would say, *I'd better be really good or else Dr. Atkins will yell at me*, while others would say, *Who the fuck does this guy think he is? I'm never coming back to this place*," said Lipson.

Atkins was well aware of this, and, while he hated to lose a patient, he never tried to alter his delivery.

So Lipson and other employees spoke with Veronica about getting Atkins to change his style, but it backfired. "She thought we were all conspiring against him," he said. So the group agreed to meet to decide what their next step would be. Since Veronica had free rein of the office, she happened to walk into the room in the middle of the meeting and Lipson explained the purpose of the discussion. He thought she could offer up some ideas, but instead she became angry and defensive, asking why Bob wasn't there and saying that the meeting wasn't necessary.

Lipson said that occasionally a staffer would complain to Atkins whenever they felt that Veronica had stuck her nose in a place where it wasn't necessary, but she stood up for him so well that he felt he should defend her just as strongly. "He'd kind of shrug, or say, 'She shouldn't have a hand in that,' but then he wouldn't say anything to her," he said. "She wanted to be an overseer of the practice and serve as his eyes and ears wherever he didn't happen to be at that moment."

In addition to having a suspicious nature, Veronica believed that since Atkins had founded the practice and had to fight so many struggles for so many years, the employees at the center were not sufficiently grateful for the sacrifices that he made. "It was like we were all sponging off him, so therefore everyone had to work harder to take care of him more, which, of course, is essentially what she was trying to do for him," said Lipson. Again, just like the strangers who visited Atkins with business plans in hand, Lipson believes that over the years Atkins had developed a sense of entitlement and felt that no one, including his own employees, would ever fully appreciate the battles he had fought for so many years,

Despite his tendency to yell at patients, in many cases Atkins had a soft spot for those who dutifully followed his instructions. If a longtime patient began to run into money problems, he would often cut him or her some slack, either cutting the bill in half or forgetting about it altogether, especially if the patient was only a couple of months away from reaching his or her ideal weight.

It's no wonder, then, that his medical practice was literally hemorrhaging money. Atkins always prided himself on a robustly staffed team, with a full roster of nurses, assistants, and physicians. By the early 1990s, he had over ninety full-time employees, including a roster of acupuncturists, massage therapists, and even herbalists.

He set his fees based on what he figured would cover his overhead, staff salaries, and no more. But between reduced patient loads and the forgiving of some patients' debt, more than a few staffers wondered how he even managed to break even, especially when the number of malpractice lawsuits filed against Atkins continued to grow.

At the time, Atkins decided that his practice needed to take preemptive action to protect itself as well, for once word got out that he was an easy mark and would quickly settle lawsuits undoubtedly more people would come to the center masquerading as patients and then easily find a lawyer who later would point a finger at some quack procedure Atkins or one of his colleagues performed. After all, when the door to the Atkins Center opened each morning at seven anyone could walk in and make an appointment; indeed, in his numerous appearances in the media each week, Atkins did everything he could to encourage that atmosphere of openness.

The problem was that this policy tended to attract a few unstable individuals from time to time, and so a better system—and a brandnew staff position—were needed to help to screen out those patients who might cause trouble down the road. This is how Len Lipson became an employee at the Atkins Center in 1990.

"My unofficial title was 'Hostility Protector,'" said Lipson, whose job was to conduct an initial interview with most of the new patients at the center and then write up a report for the patient's file.

The "Behavioral Medicine Profile," as it came to be known, would determine the amount of difficulty that Dr. Atkins or other employees might encounter with the patient. The profile detailed the kind of issues that might cause the patient to react negatively, and it provided suggestions for what to do or say to the patient to tone down an inflammatory situation. In addition, Lipson would make referrals for the kind of psychotherapy, if any, he thought would be appropriate.

Last, the Behavioral Medicine Profile included a number, from 1 to 10, that summarized the potential for difficulty so that if Atkins didn't have time to read the entire report but could look at the number, he could instantly know how much he should protect himself.

Though it wasn't a frequent occurrence, Lipson said that a patient occasionally would become so enraged at something Atkins said that the patient would lunge across the big desk to attack him. But, for the most part, Atkins didn't feel threatened by patients like this; instead, he faced the disturbance with an eerie sense of calm, even before Veronica appeared on the scene. Similarly, when an employee would express doubt or despair over disbelievers out there in the world, Atkins played the paternal, almost otherwordly leader. It seems that he had gotten through the years and years of criticism and hatred by almost assuming the persona of a cult leader.

In fact, it was common for Atkins to hire his skeptics; he actually relished the challenge. He felt that if he could win them over, there was hope for the world.

Jacqueline Eberstein, who worked side by side with Atkins for thirty years, was initially one of those nonbelievers. In her first interview with Atkins, she told him outright she thought he was a quack.

"When can you start?" he replied.

Dr. Keith Berkowitz said that the relationship Atkins had with Jackie was very unusual, because it was rare for a doctor to place that much trust in and show that much respect for someone in the nursing field. "He actually valued people who weren't doctors, and took their opinion very seriously," he said. "One thing he always joked about was if he didn't know the answer to something, ask Jackie instead."

"She was very loyal," said Bernard Raxlen. "But at the same time she could be exasperating to him, but that's a common thing, when a head nurse knows all the idiosyncracies of the doctor she works with, the good and the bad stuff. But she ran a pretty good ship when I was there, and I think she believed in him."

However, longevity among employees was not uncommon. Berkowitz said that when he first began working at the Atkins Center, most of the other staffers had ten or fifteen years' experience under their belts. "People tended to stay there a long time," he said.

"They were passionate about their work. It was more than just a job for them and I think that was amazing when I walked in and saw these people rally around this man and had gone through some kind of war with him, and still wanted to continue regardless."

Lipson agreed with his analysis of the feel of the practice. "Working at the Atkins Center almost felt like we were living in a cult," he said. "The world around us thought we were wrong and crazy, and it was an odd experience because patients would come in and be on fire because the diet was working. Their cholesterol was going down, they were losing weight and feeling better. And then we walked outside the door and people would say, 'Oh my god, you're eating fat, you're going to have a heart attack!' So we were subjected to two very different forms of reality."

And like others who headed up groups where the belief system is largely frowned upon by the outside world, Atkins kept the focus on the ultimate goal and did his best to steer the attention away from his personal life. "He seemed far more comfortable in his professional role than he did in his social role," said Lipson. "He liked talking about the diet and the issues that were making other people's lives absolutely insane. But he didn't like to talk about himself."

Robert Atkins was also exhausted from years of having patients and colleagues repeatedly ask when he was going to conduct a medical study based on his diet. Although Atkins could have financed a medical study very easily he still bristled at the suggestion, because, in his eyes, all that anybody needed to know could be found in the results he saw in his practice every day. And if a critic or traditional physician ignored his invitation to come look at the files, well, then, they didn't want to see the truth. At this point, he didn't much give a damn about what his peers thought anymore.

"He had recoiled from the traditional medical establishment from the early days because of the way they treated him when his first book came out," said Bernard Raxlen, "so I don't think he really cared anymore. He was making a ton of dough, really raking it in from his books. The other guys were running around in cubicles all day, doing all the wrong things, prescribing all kinds of toxic medicines, while he was having a great time, and people were getting better and he didn't have to poison them."

At the same time, it was quite understandable why the demand for proof was still being heard loud and clear. After all, we were taught for years that eating fat will make you fat. Atkins's theory was extremely counterintuitive to what was still being preached by nutritionists, other doctors, and even the U.S. government.

Despite this, colleagues would not let up. Raxlen continued to preach to Atkins on the necessity of having the results scientifically validated. "I told him, you have a war chest, at least get your data down and into scientific form, even if you have to pay a university or a group of researchers to do it. If you don't publish the damn stuff, you are always going to be fighting the scientific academics who will always pit their scientific paper against your bestseller, and you'll never win."

Atkins told Raxlen he was right, every bit of it. But he didn't have the time to do that kind of research. He wasn't with a university. He was a clinician. He knew something and people were getting better. As far as Atkins was concerned, that was good enough for him.

"Somebody else is going to have to do it first and it won't be me," he said.

Dr. Atkins's words would turn out to be prophetic, since somebody was already working on it.

7.

The Sweet Spot

As 1995 began, Robert Atkins was sixty-four years old and had been preaching the low-carb, high-fat gospel for more than two decades. The hardcover edition of his latest book, *Dr. Atkins' New Diet Revolution*, published in 1992, was going on its fourth year on *The New York Times* bestseller list, and though he personally was beginning to think the tide was turning his way again, he would never let on to a reporter that, through the years, he was anything less than one hundred percent certain about his diet.

A change was in the air. Maybe Americans were all getting older and wiser, but one thing was for sure: the tide was clearly turning. In the mid-'90s, people were getting awfully tired of having water-packed tuna with low-fat mayonnaise and a glass of skim milk and calling it a meal. Then there was the more frequent occurrence of garden-variety weight problems and obesity among Americans. The needle on that bathroom scale never seemed to budge as much as one wanted. And so after years of seeing Dr. Atkins relegated to a quack on everything from *Donahue* to *The Tonight Show*, battle-weary dieters began to throw away their fat-gram-counter books and really listen to what the man had to say. After all, his diet was still here after all these years. The same could not be said for the Scarsdale Diet, the Liquid Protein Diet, or the Beverly Hills Diet.

Frustrated dieters who had disparaged the Atkins Diet in the past now heard his arguments. They picked up a copy of his new book. Well, maybe it was time for a second look.

Turns out they weren't to blame for failing after all. Millions of people who religiously followed the low-fat mantra were in the same boat. Though they ate like birds, they still couldn't lose weight and keep it off. They blamed themselves for having no willpower. Yet they spent every waking hour ravenously hungry.

Happily, Atkins didn't blame them. Americans were in lockstep with what the government was telling them. And we had collectively as a people gotten fatter overall.

Perhaps most important, a few well-respected medical experts were slowly starting to come around to what Atkins had been talking about for years.

"It is important to point out that there is some element of truth to this diet," Walter Willett, M.D., the chairman of nutrition at the Harvard School of Public Health, said in 1996. "There is increasing evidence that high amounts of carbohydrates in the diet, particularly to a population that tends to be sedentary like the U.S., is not good." He tempered his optimism with concern that when it came to eating so much animal protein and fat, the jury was still out.

But for Dr. Atkins, that little bit of encouragement, coming from a Harvard chair no less, was all he needed.

Another bright spot in his life was that *New Diet Revolution* continued to sell well, and the first paperback printing, to be released in late December 1997, was set for one million copies.

Even though Atkins was thrilled with this news, his old self couldn't help but emerge.

"Well, [the publisher] *could* do two million," he said.

Even with his high profile and his money, Atkins was not about to let people take him or his message for granted. He still made the media rounds frequently, though by this point he usually made sure that a spokesperson from the Atkins Center accompanied him to appearances, to act as the voice of reason, to quell the often inflammatory words and soften the harsh suppositions that came streaming out of the doctor's mouth.

Colette Heimowitz, director of nutrition at the center, often served as Atkins's foil. When one reporter asked him if the diet was anything more than just meat and vegetables, Heimowitz stepped forward.

"It's not all about meat," she said. "The diet includes poultry, seeds, nuts, fish, eggs, and tofu."

Later, when the same reporter asked Atkins why so many physicians believed the diet was dangerous, Atkins replied, "It is quite obvious that none of them have reviewed the medical literature [and instead] speculate on what they thought might happen, which only indicates how little contact they have with reality."

Heimowitz tempered Atkins's words by explaining that most physicians and other medical professionals relied on the federal government's Food Guide Pyramid, which was originally based on food surplus. A diet including 200 grams of any kind of carbohydrate was considered healthy, according to the pyramid. "That is inappropriate for a sedentary population," she summed up.

Indeed, Heimowitz admitted that despite constantly telling Atkins to tone it down, he would still boldly announce to reporters that anyone who disagreed with him and his ideas was an "idiot."

Reporters often complained that an Atkins interview was an often boorish presentation; that he was arrogant, dismissive of anything that even slightly smacked of criticism of his life's work.

Atkins himself stressed that he always needed to bring a sidekick along to interviews. In fact, he regularly refused reporters' requests for an interview if they insisted it be with just him alone. "I don't like it when people try to put a spin and have a second agenda to make a person look bad," he once said.

But sometimes it was obvious that ever since he discovered he could attract public and press attention by saying outrageous things, it had become a natural part of him—so much so that it started to affect his speech even when he wasn't trying to shock anyone.

In 1996, while dining with a reporter and his then-sidekick/marketing director Nancy Hancock, she ordered trout wrapped in a mashed potato crust and you could hear the reporter's eyebrows go up.

"I just take off the crust," Hancock explained, and Dr. Atkins nodded.

"I've always been afraid of the potatoes, or I would have ordered it, too," he added.

A grown man admitting he's afraid of spuds would be scary

enough from the mouths of most, but Atkins, who had been fighting the battle for so long, clearly no longer cared much about what his critics said about him. And though he still preached that the only way to follow his diet was to concentrate on unprocessed foods, and still considered selling energy bars and shakes not much more than a hobby, this, too, was beginning to change. By the end of the 1990s, Atkins would be enjoying his second major wave of popularity—and the first place it was evident was his hobby.

It was no secret that the Atkins energy bars and shakes left a lot to be desired when it came to taste and texture. One staffer described the taste as being so bad it would stunt your growth. Yet despite the challenge facing the products, by 1999 the gross revenue for Atkins Nutritionals had grown to thirty-five million dollars.

Then the turn of the millennium provided just the push that Atkins needed to see the potential of the supplement side of his business. That and the raging success of one of his competitors.

In 1999, Carbolite Foods was a tiny manufacturing company that saw the low-carb market need and proceeded to develop a low-carb, low-sugar chocolate bar that actually tasted good. After only two months on the market, the bars were selling at a rate of a million a month. While 7-Eleven stores already were selling the bar, it wasn't until they listened to Carbolite's suggestion to display the bar right next to Snickers, Milky Way, and other popular candy selections that sales went through the roof.

By the end of 2000, the Carbolite bar was the third-bestselling item in the entire chain. That it actually tasted good didn't hurt sales, either.

Clearly, there was a lot of potential in Atkins's hobby, and with the growing public awareness and popularity of low-carb diets there was no time to waste.

After much agonizing about placing the future of his company in the hands of outsiders, albeit those who had significant experience in growing a company, in August of 2000 Atkins finally decided to hand over the reins so he could concentrate on his patients. At the same time, he hoped this would prove to Veronica that he was willing to cut back on his work obligations. At that time the company was marketing the energy bars and low-carb shakes only, under the brand name "Advantage," and the products were still manufactured by outside contractors.

Atkins charged executives Scott Kabak and Paul Wolff with the task of bringing the food end of the business, now christened "Atkins Nutritionals," into the clearly carb-aware twenty-first century. Kabak's previous experience was in publishing, having just served as the president of Times Mirror Magazines. Wolff worked in a variety of management positions with Kabak at Times Mirror, and he went on to launch a company that created custom publications for natural food manufacturers. In fact, he had been publishing the catalog for Atkins's line of products, which was the major reason Atkins approached him to run the company.

After the two men and Atkins reached an agreement, he essentially told them to run with it and develop the business as they saw fit. While press reports announced that Kabak and Wolff were running Atkins Nutritionals, the truth is they were actually running the entire Atkins empire, including the Atkins Center. Done with

Atkins's blessing, he no doubt suffered a great deal of personal angst. After all, it was his baby.

Once on board, Kabak and Wolff started delineating the sometimes outrageous reputation of Atkins the man from Atkins the business, including the publishing side of the empire. Even though books written by Atkins were published by other companies, they were able to convince publisher St. Martin's Press that the forthcoming *Atkins for Life* be the doctor's first book not to feature his picture on the jacket.

As Wolff put it, "We have transcended fad."

Despite the fact that Robert Atkins no longer called the shots, he still was the official spokesman for the company, and he was trotted out whenever a new product was introduced, or whenever a reporter wanted to write a feature story on the newly revamped Atkins Center. When he signed over control of the company, it almost seems like he had to agree to a keep a lower profile, in order not to criticize the goose that was laying the golden egg, because while he still made outrageous statements to the press he never complained about the direction the empire was headed.

Longtime colleagues sensed Veronica Atkins's hand in this arrangement, as she had taken a keen interest in the food and supplement side of the business since they were married. They believed that it was her idea initially to change the direction of the company by curtailing her husband's involvement; after all, it would be one way to force him to retire, or at least cut down on the hours he spent working. From the day that Kabak and Wolff came on board, Veronica began to work very closely with the two, and it quickly became apparent that their vision for the company matched hers. Again, Atkins could care less. As long as he could still work with his patients he was happy.

In 2001, the aggressiveness of the executives' new plan was evident in the rapid growth of the business. Before Wolff and Kabak arrived, the catalog was published and mailed erratically, anywhere from four to six times a year. But starting in 2002, it would be sent eight times yearly, and on very a strict schedule. In addition, while in the past the number of new products introduced in each catalog averaged around five, now it was twenty-five to thirty. The catalog offered a mix of Atkins and outside-manufacturered products, though as the number of new Atkins label products increased the number offered by outside manufacturers decreased. After all, more money could be made manufacturing in-house than out.

"The opportunity for us was to take a concept and make it a brand," said chairman and CEO Paul Wolff. In fact, the goal was to transform the Atkins name from diet doctor to dietary lifestyle.

Matthew Wiant, senior vice president at the company, reiterated this belief. "It's important to quickly make the brand transcend the individual," he said, "to make it stand for an approach to eating as opposed to representing just one man. [Atkins] was the catalyst, but the movement has gotten big enough that it's going to perpetuate itself."

Dean Rotbart, who in 2003 founded *LowCarbiz*, an industry publication that follows the burgeoning low-carb-food industry, agrees. "Atkins has become something like [what] Kleenex is to facial tissue."

Certainly, the growing, though conditional, acceptance by the medical community was just beginning to surface around this time.

In addition to the Harvard physician who publicly attested to the validity of the science behind the Atkins diet, albeit with reservations several more-mainstream physicians—including some holding high-level positions at renowned teaching hospitals—began to concur with what Atkins had been preaching for three decades. As a result, his reputation began to improve in an "I told two friends, and they told two friends" kind of way. It was especially effective here because of the caliber of the physicians passing along the word. Through the second half of the 1990s, it could having been simply achieving critical mass that finally tipped the balance toward Atkins.

"I think what made him happiest was when he finally got to speak in places like Cornell," said Keith Berkowitz, who worked with Atkins in 2003. "After all, it was where he had trained, but his ideas were never accepted by mainstream medicine. Yet he finally got the opportunity to lecture there and the people applauded him."

It had to have felt wonderful to be vindicated after being not much more than a punching bag for his critics for so many years. Atkins went from being the most unpopular kid in the class to the doctor who had maintained his position for decades in the face of great opposition.

Yet he still couldn't resist baiting his critics. After all, old habits die hard.

In 2000, he gave a talk at the annual convention of the American Dietetic Association, a group that had opposed his ideas from the beginning. But since his fortunes were beginning to turn, he approached the occasion with humor. "I'm very happy to be here, but not as happy as Daniel in the lion's den," he cracked.

Still, as tolerance and outright acceptance of Atkins's ideas grew, even in his later years his bitterness toward the medical establishment came through loud and clear. When an audience member in an on-line forum told Dr. Atkins that her doctor ordered her to "get off" the diet, he fired back, "I strongly recommend that you get off the relationship you have with your doctor." Once again, with Colette Heimowitz at his side, she cushioned his words with an unemotionally charged explanation that helped tone him down.

And while he had admitted, "There is no question that of all the thousands of studies published, people can use selective citation to prove anything they want," the writing was on the wall, and he surprised everyone by finally agreeing it was time to conduct an official medical study of his diet.

Slowly, with enough patients convincing their doctors that the diet worked, and then with those doctors trying the diet themselves, mainstream physicians all over the country, some at major medical institutions, began to take a closer look at the low-carb regimen. One in particular, Eric Westman, a professor of medicine at Duke University Medical Center and a general internist, was so skeptical initially that he didn't believe Atkins actually had gone to medical school and earned his M.D.

Back in 1997, Westman had been treating several patients who lost a lot of weight on the Atkins diet while he was the director of the smoking research laboratory. He had little expertise when it came to weight loss, so he knew next to nothing about low-carb diets. His patients recommended that he read *New Diet Revolution*. It took several months, but he finally did.

After Westman finished the book, and after seeing the results in his own patients, he still didn't believe that the diet worked, and that their cholesterol levels would go down because of all the meat they were eating. "One patient ate nothing but steak and eggs and lost about thirty pounds," he said. "I told him that I had to check his cholesterol, because I was sure it had gone up. Well, it had actually gotten better."

Still puzzled, Westman decided to send Atkins a letter describing his experiences, ending by saying that he couldn't understand why the diet worked when it went against what everyone believed and what studies up until then maintained. After he mailed the letter, Westman forgot about it, until one day the phone rang and it was Atkins on the line.

"I explained my quandary again, then told him I need data, I need proof that this works," said Westman.

Atkins countered by saying it was all in the book.

"I told him that I read the book," Westman said, "and there are plenty of anecdotes in the book, but that's not good enough for science. Then he said, 'Why would I want to fund any research when I already know what the results will be?'"

Westman explained that was all well and good, but no one else would believe it unless it was presented in a formal study.

"You need someone to do the research," Westman said, adding that he was interested since he had observed it in his own patients.

And so Atkins invited Westman to come to New York to observe the clinic and sit in on some sessions with patients. Westman liked what he saw, put together a proposal with the understanding that Atkins would provide the funding for the study to be conducted, and together they came up with a schedule. Two years later, the study got off the ground.

What's particularly interesting is that it wasn't until Westman actually visited the center and spent time with Atkins and his patients and staff that he was convinced that Atkins was less of a quack that the media and his critics had painted him to be.

"I was both surprised and impressed that he actually had an office and was seeing patients," Westman said. "I had to see through the veneer of the book before I could actually start to believe the concept behind the diet."

Westman put fifty people on the Atkins diet and followed their progress for six months. He followed the same protocol that patients at the center followed: first, they went on the induction phase of the diet; then they took the same nutritional supplements that patients took at the center.

As Atkins had predicted, Westman's patients lost weight, and, for the most part, their cholesterol levels were down. When Westman presented the results of the study to Atkins, of course Atkins said he wasn't surprised. Westman said he was intrigued by the findings but that the next logical step was to conduct another study. When Atkins balked, he explained.

First, a second study that validates the results of the first is very important in order to establish scientific credibility. That is, researchers need to come up with the exact same results a second time. Plus, they also needed to have a control group following another diet, such as the low-fat diet recommended by the American Heart Association at the time.

After his initial reservation, Atkins agreed. Again, he and Westman hashed out the details. The second study was undertaken in 2001. The results validated those of the first study. Again, just as Atkins had predicted.

The positive news about the studies happened to dovetail nicely with the aims of Atkins Nutritionals and the desire of Scott Kabak and Paul Wolff to expand the company exponentially. While Atkins obviously wanted acceptance from the medical community that had lambasted him for decades, there was another compelling reason the studies would come in handy: from the beginning of their tenure, Kabak and Wolff wanted every product that bore the Atkins name to be "rooted in science." This is the reason for all the small print that appears on the packaging, in pamphlets, and on the Web site.

Despite Atkins's ascent and validation from the medical community, he still wasn't satisfied. Perhaps these initial small affirmations couldn't begin to make up for the years of criticism and constant struggle, but, more likely, the reason was the same as with every other area of his life where he didn't feel he could ever have enough: it was family tradition. His feelings were only exacerbated when his mother, Norma, came to New York to visit him. He had bought her apartments, houses, paid her bills, yet she still criticized him. After all, she had taught him from childhood that enough would never be enough. Plus, as her only son, he had never provided her with grandchildren, something she would always regret.

Atkins usually didn't talk about his family, but occasionally a reporter would ask him why his mother was overweight. He would play the downtrodden son in an exaggerated manner, sigh loudly, shrug his shoulders, and say with resignation, "She cheats."

According to one longtime colleague, "Norma was a trip. She'd come up from Florida, and we would have to chauffeur her around and take her shopping, and even in the late 1990s, she'd still say she wished her son would become a real doctor." It could have been she worried about him as a mother or because her son couldn't stop pushing beyond the boundaries while her friends' sons were also successful but didn't feel the need to constantly rock the boat. Or maybe it was a combination of the two.

Those who had known Atkins for a long time began to see changes in him, and not always for the better. As he got older, some said that he became more like himself, a caricature of his earlier, more obnoxious self. And the critics, relentless as ever, were still taking their toll on him.

Since Atkins still relished a good fight, even though both the frequency and ferocity were beginning to decrease, he relied on his old standby of sarcasm whenever he wanted to stir things up.

He still parlayed the colorful anecdote to illustrate his point, or he'd take a new point of view whenever a journalist asked him a question he'd been hearing for years.

"Sixty more years to live," he told CNN in January 2003 when a reporter asked what he thought about the typical low-fat diet and the longevity promised as a result. "Are they going to go hungry for all sixty years?"

He also liked to play around with words in an interview, but he could sometimes be a bit sloppy when he did.

"We reverse heart disease all the time," he told Larry King on his show in January 2003.

"That, I'm told, is impossible," King responded. "I mean, you can control it, but you can't reverse it."

"Well, a lot of people who have been told that they need bypass come to us."

"And you take the blockage away?" asked an incredulous King.

"Well, we took away the symptom complex. And the cardiologists who told them they needed a bypass reevaluated them and said, well, I guess you don't because everything's okay."

A sharp dresser, his preferred dress of dapper jacket and tasseled loafers seemed out of date, but, then again, Dr. Atkins was often a throwback to an earlier era.

He still didn't pay much attention to what was considered to be in style at any given time. As a result, he was hopelessly dated and considered under the radar by the social set. They even thought his house was located on the wrong side of the Hamptons. One snooty hipster referred to his house as "so late-seventies."

Once low-carb became all the rage in the Hamptons and elsewhere, his out-of-touch-ness mattered not a whit to the stylish set. Atkins was invited to a pool party and showed up in slacks, but, instead of snickering at his total lack of fashion sense, the partygoers became all flustered and started to grab at anything on the buffet table that had even one gram of carbohydrate in it so they could hide it from him.

*   *   *

When Atkins appeared on MSNBC's *Phil Donahue Show* on January 29, 2003, Donahue presented the American Heart Association's boilerplate criticism of the Atkins diet and asked for his response. Atkins replied that the group's seal of approval regularly appeared on packaged foods that were essentially comprised of half sugar and half white flour—what most people regard as junk food.

"It's an honor to have people like that be my critics," he retorted.

Later in the interview, Atkins took the opportunity to plug for alternative medicine while slamming traditional medicine. He explained that such commonly prescribed hormones as estrogen and progestin are the primary cause of weight gain among postmenopausal woman. "The trick, I guess, is to hide under the bed," he joked.

His long-standing feuds with diet doctors and nutritionists who were 180 degrees on the other side of the low-carb lifestyle also continued. In several cases, his critics became even more vociferous when Atkins became more popular and his diet started to be accepted.

His antipathy toward Dr. Dean Ornish, who played low-fat devil's advocate to Atkins's steak-and-cheese siren song, ramped up a few notches. As was the case with the Atkins-Pritikin feud two decades earlier, radio and TV producers loved to play one off the other. The matchup was also popular on conference circuit, where their debating likely would be the most energetic offering in a series of otherwise tedious presentations.

Drs. Atkins and Ornish duked it out at the annual conference of the American College of Cardiology in Orlando in the spring of 2001. It only took a minute or two for the gloves to come off once they were introduced to the audience. Dr. Ornish spoke first.

"I think the burden of proof is first to do the studies showing something works, and then do the books recommending that people follow it," he said, "and not the other way around."

Atkins's retort: "Dr. Ornish is hooked on the idea that the proof hasn't come yet, and I agree. At the same time, it is quite obvious from all of the other studies that are related to it that the proof will come, and it will work out the way it does in the clinical practice of medicine."

A few months before Robert Atkins died, he got in a few final words about his most vociferous critic. "I don't think Dean Ornish has ever read my book. He still goes around telling people that my diet is all fried pork rinds. Dean Ornish is so determined to make me look bad, he doesn't even know that fried pork rinds are actually very low in fat."

Atkins didn't often cook—that was Veronica's job and passion—but when he did, he specialized in what he called "Internalized Cheeseburgers."

He described how to make them to John Hockenberry of *Dateline NBC*, who interviewed him six weeks before he died.

"I put all the meat on the outside, divide them in half, put the cheese on the inside, put them together, and flip them over," he said. "The cheese melts on the inside and never gets out."

Hockenberry's response: "You might call that an 'Atkins cruise missile.'"

Even though Dr. Atkins steadfastly remained dedicated to

spreading the low-carb gospel, it didn't mean the diet he promoted remained the same over the years. Particularly after Veronica entered his life and began to serve as his coauthor on the cookbooks, he began to recommend foods for the maintenance phase of the diet that may have had a few more grams of carbohydrate than were allowed in his first book; however, the additional grams usually were from whole grains, never from refined sugar or white flour.

Even in 2001, Atkins began to alter his message slightly, perhaps owing to the fact that as he grew older and his overall health began to decline he discovered that he could no longer eat his beloved low-carb diet with total abandon as he once could. And so at public appearances and in his books, he began discussing such issues as controlling portion size, the importance of antioxidants and the need for exercise, and other commonsense health approaches, which, five or ten years earlier, he would have undoubtedly dismissed with a wave of the hand.

And yet, two months before his death, Atkins would still say things like, "I believe pasta is a junk food."

Ron Arky remembers one late-night phone call he received from Robert Atkins in 2001, when his old medical school buddy sounded out of sorts.

"He sounded really depressed," Arky said, adding that while emotional problems were out of the realm of his specialty, "if I was taping that conversation as a clinician, I would say, boy, this guy is really depressed."

Not only the press noticed but even total strangers. In 2001, during a stint as the featured speaker at a conference on obesity in a

Detroit suburb, *Free Press* reporter Ellen Creager noted that Atkins "looked a little tired . . . he had dark circles under his eyes and seemed not quite robust." Craeger describes how Atkins had tried to cancel his appearance at the conference, blaming a slight case of pneumonia and a sore ankle, but when the promoter told Atkins he would provide a private jet and door-to-door limo service he acquiesced and agreed to attend.

In a way, even though he could well afford these luxuries for himself, the fact that a conference presenter wanted him to come badly enough to shell out significantly must have appealed to Atkins's sense of pride, his sense of importance, and he just couldn't turn them down. Even with broad acceptance of his diet, it's clear that he still would respond to a little flattery. Anything to bring him out of his funk in this new world where his ideas were welcome—embraced, even—but where he was becoming increasingly superfluous. The only one pleased with this development, besides the executives at Atkins, would be Veronica. After all, she could spend more time with him.

The truth was, the Atkins Center, his pride and joy, his baby, would soon be a shadow of its former self.

Nobody saw it coming. Not even Robert Atkins.

With the practice and supplement business both safely tucked under the umbrella of the newly formed Atkins Nutritionals, Inc., the people now calling the shots were two outsiders who viewed the company solely as a moneymaker with unlimited potential as long as the low-carb frenzy continued to snowball. The medical practice, on the other hand, was a money loser. Atkins still had to step in himself and take money out of his own pocket whenever accounts grew perilously low and at the end of each fiscal year to balance the books.

A major housecleaning was clearly in order, and it happened quickly. Before the smoke cleared, the center went from its all-time high of about ninety employees down to fourteen in a matter of weeks.

According to several employees who lost their jobs, a couple of people from the accounting department prepared profit-and-loss statements for each of the center's departments including all alternative treatments, such as acupuncture and chiropractic adjustment, as well as supplements sold to patients at the center. All of the departments, except for the supplements, were losing money, according to the figures.

That came as no surprise to longtime employees; it had been an open secret for years. Aside from Atkins personally balancing the books, the unspoken dictate was to always sell a couple more supplements to each patient and at least it wouldn't be as bad.

But this time was different. The new corporate administration believed that the chronic loss of money had gone on for too long, and it would not be tolerated any longer. Instead of giving each department a period of probation in which to break even, or at least reduce the hemorrhaging to a mere trickle, most of the employees were given the ax without recourse to appeal. Several cut employees accused the company of manipulating the numbers to make the losses appear much worse than they actually were, but the charge wouldn't stick. And, besides, the powers that be obviously had made up their minds already.

Technically, they felt that Atkins Nutritionals was supplementing the practice, and they didn't want it to continue because the practice was not vital to the growth of the business overall. To put it bluntly, the Atkins Center was becoming an albatross around the neck of Atkins Nutritionals.

Robert Atkins never spoke about the incident publicly—it wasn't publicized at the time—but he must have been heartbroken. He still had his patients, of course, but with the reduced staff it would take longer for them to get appointments, so many would have no choice but to go elsewhere.

"My understanding was that Dr. Atkins was not happy with this," said employee Len Lipson. "I never had a direct conversation with him about it, as I was gone by that point, but I do know there was some conflict between him and the executives over what was happening with his baby."

In retrospect, it should come as no surprise that since Dr. Atkins lost control of his practice and his business he would want to come up with a way to ensure that his ideas and influence could extend beyond a shelf full of packaged, highly processed food. Again, coincidental to the studies validating what he preached for so many years, Atkins decided to fund a foundation having no connection to the company whatsoever, where he could continue to validate his ideas. If he set up the foundation properly, his influence would continue long after he was gone.

And so the Atkins Foundation was born. The beginnings were rather small, with just Atkins, Veronica, and an administrator to run it. Their initial purpose was to fund studies that would scientifically prove that a low-carb diet was beneficial for long-term weight loss, and that it caused cholesterol levels to drop. One of the first projects the foundation funded was Westman's second study.

Once the first few studies passed muster, Atkins decided it was time to bring in a seasoned researcher, in addition to the administrator. Abby Bloch, Ph.D., had developed a successful nutrition consultancy by the time Atkins got in touch with her about coming to work at the foundation. Dr. Bloch made no secret of her distaste for low-carb diets. Despite her reservations, she was hired to approve studies for funding and review research protocols.

It took some time for Bloch to get over her shock at Atkins hiring her, a nonbeliever. "It impressed me that even though I had very boldly expressed my pessimism and disbelief when it came to the diet, he was still comfortable enough to tell me as long as I was willing to actually look at the data with an open mind, he would take me on," she said. "He got a kick out of seeing me change my belief system, and it was exciting for me to begin to see how his theories were validated through the studies."

Abby Bloch almost didn't make it through the door of the center the first day, however, when she realized that this large medical organization, on six floors of a midtown office building, was essentially run, in her words, as "a mom-and-pop operation." Despite the notoriety Atkins had engendered over the years, Bloch went to the job interview with a very different picture in mind.

"I had imagined him as this high-powered, very focused businessman, when his real commitment and love were reserved for the center and his patients," she said. Or at least what remained of the center at that time.

Despite their seemingly divergent paths—he was a pure clinician, she had always done research—Dr. Bloch says that their relationship thrived. "We had a great relationship. He respected my clinical research background while I respected his clinical management and what he was able to achieve with his patients," she said.

While the primary goal of those early studies was simply to validate the science behind a low-carb diet, Atkins knew that the only way the medical community would sit up and take notice was for the foundation to be totally hands off with the studies, bucking the trend when it came to the majority of medical studies conducted in the early twenty-first century. Government agencies at one time were very generous in funding medical research. But as federal money got tighter with overburdened budgets, more researchers began to pursue private funding sources, particularly drug companies.

Dr. Bloch explained that the pharmaceutical companies keep a tight handle on not only how the money is spent but also how the results were reported. If it looked like a study would end up with a conclusion that would reflect poorly on a particular drug or therapy, more often than not the study would end prematurely, and all data from the study kept confidential. As part of the agreement to receive funding, in fact, researchers are required to sign a contract which stipulates that they agree to keep silent about the results.

So while Atkins's decision to totally detach himself and the foundation from the studies the foundation funded was quite revolutionary, it was also quite necessary, to ensure that no one could accuse researchers of being in Atkins's pocket. In fact, one respected researcher, George L. Blackburn, M.D., Ph.D., who is affiliated with Beth Israel Deaconness Medical Center in Boston, was surprised. "He was accustomed to abiding by the dictates of industry-funded research," said Dr. Bloch, "and once his study for the Atkins Foundation began, he was pleasantly surprised at how hands off we were."

Probably for the first time in his life, Robert Atkins kept quiet when it came to research, after years of railing about how useless he thought it was. That's because he was beginning to view the foundation as his legacy. "He recognized that he was getting on in years, and he and Veronica had no children or family," said Bloch. "He recognized that if his message was going to reach beyond his patients and his committed fan base, he had to get the medical establishment to accept what he already clinically knew was possible." It may have taken Atkins several decades, but he finally recognized that it would only be through the research that others would be willing to begin to look at the benefits of a low-carb diet seriously.

Despite this giant step forward, the critics were still lurking. "They used to criticize me for not funding a study," Atkins later said. "So when we got some money together and we were able to do it, then they criticized me for funding a study. But the most important thing is that there were eight other studies that we didn't fund that showed exactly the same thing. Some of them were even done by people who were our critics," a fact which must have afforded him a great deal of satisfaction.

So while he was extremely saddened at the radical downscaling of his practice, he was heartened at the promise of the foundation.

Things were finally looking up for the future. Then, on Thursday, April 18, 2002, something happened that could have stopped the growing approval of a low-carb diet in its tracks, despite all of the positive studies.

Dr. Atkins had a heart attack, or, more specifically, he suffered cardiac arrest while eating breakfast. His longtime nurse, Jackie Eberstein, resuscitated him by giving him CPR and mouth-to-mouth while waiting for the ambulance to arrive.

He stayed in the hospital for a full week, and then made an appearance on *The Today Show* to assure his fans and disparage his critics, though, admittedly, he did look tired and pale.

As expected, Atkins's critics came out of the woodwork to point to his diet as the cause, and even his staunchest fans—his patients—began to worry. Both Atkins and his personal cardiologist, Patrick Fratellone, M.D., assured the public that the cardiac arrest was not due to diet but an infection that he had picked up a couple of years earlier when he and Veronica had taken a long-overdue vacation overseas.

Warren Levin said that Atkins recovered fully, which is unusual for people in their seventies. "The people who said that this was a manifestation of diet totally missed the fact that his was a miraculous recovery," he said.

While Atkins's recovery was indeed a wonder, the truth is that the real miracle was just around the corner.

8.

THE PLANETS ALIGN: JULY 7, 2002

D espite a blip following Robert Atkins's heart attack, low-carb mania continued to spread like wildfire throughout the country, and around the world as well. And when he happened to stumble upon his own celebrity in unexpected places, clearly he was absolutely delighted.

Stuart Trager, a physician, began investigating the Atkins diet on his own. He invited Atkins and Veronica to a party at his Pennsylvania home to celebrate the opening of a wellness program at a Philadelphia hospital. Trager asked his wife to go through one of Atkins's cookbooks and select a variety of dishes for the caterer to prepare. This thoughtfulness allowed Atkins to eat anything he wanted, usually difficult at best at most functions he attended.

"It was very funny to hear Atkins say halfway through the cocktail hour how nice it was to go to an event where he could eat everything that was there," said Trager, who could relate somewhat to Atkins's predicament. Once he himself became associated with a low-carb diet, and especially because he was a physician, "People who used to enjoy eating a meal began to hide their plates from me at the table."

Then, the most unexpected thing happened, and it was almost too good to be true.

On Sunday, July 7, 2002, the *New York Times Magazine* cover featured a close-up of a big, juicy rare steak, headlined "What If It's All Been a Big Fat Lie?" The story, running almost eight thousand words, was written by journalist Gary Taubes. He threw it right out there for the whole world to see:

Dr. Atkins is right after all because these scientists say he is.

Despite decades of working with media of every stripe, Atkins had never experienced anything like this, and there it was, full-color, right there on the cover of the weekly magazine of the most prominent national newspaper. This, of course, was *the* watershed moment of his entire life. After decades of being on the receiving end of endless criticism and abuse from the medical community and others, here was *The New York Times* blessing the ideas he had fought for all his life.

Perhaps the most compelling aspect of the story was Taubes's getting the top names in the weight-loss field to talk. Albert Stunkard, M.D., a professor of psychiatry at the University of Pennsylvania School of Medicine and author of numerous books on obesity and eating disorders, told the journalist that for years he and his colleagues had regarded Robert Atkins as "a jerk" whose primary motivation was to become rich. Stunkard changed his mind when the chief of radiology at his hospital lost sixty pounds on Atkins's low-carb diet. Investigating further, he found other colleagues who were following the Atkins plan, losing significant amounts of weight, and feeling none the worse the wear.

"Apparently, all the young guys in the hospital are doing it," Stunkard told Taubes, "so we decided to do a study."

Stunkard's study was cited in the article, along with several others, and though reservations were expressed here and there the bottom line was that Atkins had it right and the low-fat proponents—along with the federal government—were way off track because they were ignoring science.

Atkins's colleague Fred Pescatore visited him at the Hamptons estate the afternoon the story came out. "The phone didn't stop ringing the whole time I was there," he said. "I asked Atkins how he was going to celebrate, and he said he was going to see his patients the next morning, and that was all the celebration he needed."

Of course Atkins was pleased by all the attention and approval, and after Taubes's story came out he could have done anything. But Atkins was content to let things stay just the way they were so he could focus on his patients, crank out a few more books, and work with the foundation to fund more research that would support the science behind the diet, and improve the health of people who follow it.

Not surprisingly, this overnight success didn't really change Atkins. If anything, it gave him an excuse to shuck his interpreting, mollifying sidekick on future interviews with the media. Now he was not just cantankerous as always, he was more so, and he started using the same brand of bullying he used in his practice.

"That's 'Dumb Start'!" he berated a caller to a radio show who told him she had eaten a bowl of Smart Start cereal that morning. "Oh my God! Stop eating carbohydrates!"

But at Atkins Nutritionals, things were about to change in a big way. The day after the *Times* story came out, the atmosphere there and at the Atkins Center was, as expected, charged. Employees were walking around with big smiles on their faces, knowing that something big was about to happen, that the lives they led on the Friday before were radically different today.

"The conversation is about to change," Paul Wolff said he remembered thinking that day. "You adjust your strategy and dream a little bigger." The first thing he did was to arrange for the company to purchase the rights to Gary Taubes's story, and then to plaster it everywhere they could, including on the company's Web site, and sending it out to retail outlets carrying Atkins products.

Though the research and development department at Atkins Nutritionals had already been ramped up in response to the double-digit growth in the low-carb market over the previous few years, in the wake of the *Times* story all hell broke loose and the charge from the executive suite was to move full speed ahead.

After Atkins signed over control of the center and the products, he seemingly came to a grudging acceptance of his decision, or at least he'd made his peace with it. For one thing, at least the food tasted a lot better now than when he was running it as a part-time venture.

A former colleague says that Atkins particularly liked the Crunchers, a snack that is similar to a potato chip. "He would get hungry around three o'clock, and by that point the corporate offices were in another building. So he used to come wandering by looking for something to eat, and most of the time he picked up a bag of the Crunchers."

Gary Taubes said that when he was working on the *Times* article, Atkins Nutritionals sent him a box filled with a variety of the products currently available. "When I mentioned this to him [Atkins] in the interview, he basically told me that the pasta was inedible. Whatever else they said about him, at least he was actually intellectually honest."

Taubes added that the current line of food products had become significantly better since his interview with Atkins in 2002, and he attributed it to the improved technology involved in making low-carb foods look like and taste like their high-carb counterparts.

But by the end of 2002, it was clear that Dr. Atkins wasn't entirely comfortable with the direction the company was taking in developing and marketing a bevy of new, processed food products, since he always had and still was preaching the gospel of unprocessed food. After all, he consistently told patients and readers alike that the only way you change your body is to change the way you eat. Substituting a processed low-carb food for a processed high-carb food didn't fit his philosophy.

Yet, at the same time, the reason he had introduced the energy bars and shakes in the first place was because he understood what people liked to eat, and he didn't want them to suffer as a result of following his diet. So while his uneasiness persisted, he nonetheless was thrilled just by the changes he saw in his own backyard.

Several weeks after the *Times* article came out, the culinary scene in New York City, as elsewhere in the country, was already undergoing a radical transformation. People from all walks of society were seeing food that contained refined sugar or white flour as the devil incarnate.

"It's almost hostile to serve pasta these days because so many people are on Atkins," said psychiatrist and socialite Samantha Boardman.

Jodi Balkan, a public relations executive in New York, concurred. She said she had tried low-carb diets through the years but never thought she could stay on it for life. "You always felt there was something innately wrong with it. The article in the *Times* changed my thinking, [it was] the greatest story ever."

The glowing article was followed by similar accolades just a few months later. In the fall of 2002, a study at the University of Cincinnati reported that not only did subjects lose weight faster on a low-carb diet than on a low-fat diet, they also experienced radical cardiovascular improvement, most notably in lower triglyceride levels.

The delicious irony of this study is that it was funded by one of Atkins's longest and loudest enemies, the American Heart Association. Furthermore, the research was conducted in his native state of Ohio.

Atkins was delighted, as were his medical colleagues. "What I am hearing is that people are thrilled that this is about science," said Stuart Trager. "People want believable science, and they want to hear it from someone who is objective and is both approachable and believable. I think individuals can become more confident in following a strategy that is supported by science."

After the magazine came out and the accolades poured in, Atkins changed his practice little. In a way, he still operated as if the downscaling never happened the year before. People who called the center for the first time were tickled when they heard the following recording:

"I'm Dr. Robert Atkins. We here at the Atkins Center are here to keep you healthy! If you would like information about becoming a patient at the center, please press one."

One person compared it to calling the lab of Albert Einstein and hearing the scientist himself telling callers to press 1 if they wanted to know more about the theory of relativity.

Surprisingly, despite the newfound popularity of everything Atkins, as well as the supposed increased efficiency of the practice, money was still hemorrhaging month in and month out. As before, Atkins publicly maintained that it was due to the insurance companies' refusal to pay for what they consider unorthodox medical procedures conducted at the center. A standard examination including tests ran well over a thousand dollars, and most insurance companies wouldn't reimburse patients.

"They have him flagged as an alternative physician," Colette Heimowitz told the Knight Ridder News Service in late 2002. "The research has finally caught up with his ideas, but the insurers don't care. They still treat him like a pariah."

Atkins also maintained his active schedule delivering lectures and attending medical conferences, though now he was discovering that his reception was decidedly warmer. In the fall of 2002, he was invited to speak at the annual meeting of the American Society of

Bariatric Physicians in Boston. At a gathering with colleagues just months earlier, he had been greeted with hostility, neutrality at best. But these colleagues took a different tone. Dr. Ron Arky attended his friend's lecture and was amazed at the sincerity aimed at Atkins.

"For the first time, at this conference the room was packed with doctors who were listening and were actually very interested in what he had to say," he said. "These are people who treat overweight patients on a full time basis, so they were very open to the low-carb concept, and they actually asked very intelligent questions as opposed to just being inflammatory. I know it took Dr. Atkins by surprise."

Though Arky did have differences with Atkins through the almost fifty years of their acquaintance, he clearly respected the man for his perseverance. Arky also tells a poignant story that stems from his position on the publications committee of the Massachusetts Medical Society, which oversees the *New England Journal of Medicine*.

In February 2003, a paper reporting the results of a study of low-carb diets had just come in to the journal for Arky's review, slated for publication in the May 2003 issue. "There were some very impressive data," he said, "and somebody had actually done a controlled study using his diet which confirmed some of the things he had been saying all these years." The two doctors had still kept up their periodic late-night phone calls, and Atkins happened to call a few days after Arky had read the study.

"When he called, I was so tempted to tell Bob about the upcoming publication, but that would have been highly unethical. You just don't do that once the paper has been submitted. So he never got to see the report."

*   *   *

Though it was hardly necessary for him to make the talk show circuit, Robert Atkins dove in to a full schedule of media appearances while carrying a full patient load, writing his next book, and promoting Atkins Nutritionals. Unlike before, however, it seemed that his motivation for making media appearances was to relish the victory, and maybe rub it in the faces of his critics just a little.

In early January 2003, Dr. Atkins made what would turn out to be the last of his numerous appearances on the *Larry King Show* on CNN. Throughout the interview, it was apparent that King was playing devil's advocate, possibly due to his own experience. He had had several heart attacks and undergone quintuple-bypass surgery, and in his 1989 book, *Mr. King, You're Having a Heart Attack,* he describes how a low-fat diet saved his life.

If the audience picked up on King's skepticism, it was clear when they called in that they didn't much care. All they wanted to ask Atkins was what he ate, and, therefore, what should they eat.

Despite gushing praise from callers, about halfway through the show King began challenging Atkins.

"It's very hard to get people to think that high fat is good . . . because fat is a bad word," King argued. "Fat means fat. I'll be fat if I eat fat."

Atkins responded with his boilerplate explanation tracing the obesity and diabetes epidemic back to the day the government recommended that Americans eat more carbohydrates. King parried a few times more, but he knew he was beat.

Even though Atkins promised Veronica he would cut back on

his workload—and actually was doing just that—he still had big plans for the future. He envisioned one day cutting the ribbon to his own facility on Long Island, patterned after the Atkins Center in Manhattan but vastly expanded to serve as a hospital concentrating on complementary medicine. He also planned to conduct seminars in the Hamptons house for physicians interested in including alternative services in their practices.

"Why would I give up? I'm on the verge of succeeding," he said.

Atkins basked in the accolades from public and professionals alike, but, unfortunately, he wouldn't get the chance to bask much longer.

9.

THE LAST DAYS

After years of automatically assuming a boxer's stance in every area of his professional life, Robert Atkins was taking off the gloves. He was in his element, and he was reveling in the attention. Life was good.

And then something peculiar began to happen. Dr. Atkins, the go-getter, the workaholic, the one-man low-carb preaching machine, was starting to wind down. Of course, cutting his workload by even as much as a third would still be a back-breaking load for most people. But after years of hearing his wife and others beg him to slow down, cut back, start to relax a bit—after all, he was now seventy-two years old—he stunned his nearest and dearest by announcing that the time had come to ease off a little. Veronica was thrilled.

Though he last saw Atkins in 2001, Len Lipson said that the subsequent change in Atkins's attitude as he became less combative made perfect sense. "When you get that kind of consistent pressure from all sides you have to do something to protect yourself. It was probably very subtle, but this guy had absolutely been shaped by the battle he had fought through the years, and once he no longer had a reason to fight, he had no choice but to change."

It's as though Atkins spent the better part of three decades banging his head against the wall and then he suddenly stopped. The silence must have been deafening. Many people lose their motivation for getting up in the morning when this happens, because they haven't a clue how to fill their days. It's frightening.

He nonetheless began to slack off, at least by his standards. In fact, on April 6, 2003, Atkins was flying back from a Palm Beach weekend with his friends Bob Meister, vice chairman of Aon Corporation, and Steve Ross, CEO of the Related Companies, on Ross's Gulfstream. Meister recalled that Atkins was unusually contemplative. Goldman Sachs, along with a group of several other investors, had just offered him $533 million for Atkins Nutritionals, of which 80 percent was for his personal stake in the company.

Atkins was flabbergasted by the offer. He couldn't believe that the company that he still considered to be a hobby would be worth that much money. The general consensus was that Atkins should accept, but, as was his custom, he soon started talking about patients and diagnoses, and he reverted to his usual animated self.

"Bob was never interested in pursuing money," said Meister. "It was frustrating to all of us."

Even though he had anticipated the worst when first thinking about cutting back on work, he was pleasantly surprised that he was actually looking forward to it. In fact, the very next day—April 7— Atkins Nutritionals CEO Paul Wolff said that Bob had commented on the forward-looking direction of the company.

"I gotta tell you," Wolff said Atkins told him, "I've never been happier." Wolff then said that Atkins felt that the company and its employees were as committed to making his decades-long vision a reality as he was, something that heartened him immensely.

The next day, tragedy struck.

Since Keith Berkowitz had started working at the Atkins Center a month earlier, he discovered that he and Atkins usually arrived at the front door each morning at just about the same time. On Tuesday, April 8, Berkowitz had gotten a bit of a late start, and, as he neared the building, he noticed a strange sight: a group of people were gathered in front, forming a huddle, seemingly fascinated by something on the ground. Two of them, though dressed expensively for the office, were not wearing coats.

"I saw a bag off to the side that looked very familiar to me," Berkowitz said. "That's when I realized everyone was hunched over Dr. Atkins, who was lying on the ground. I was pretty horrified."

Berkowitz rushed to Atkins's side and saw that he was bleeding profusely from the back of his head. The two people without coats had wrapped their garments around the doctor in an attempt to keep him warm while he lay on the cold, wet sidewalk. He said that Atkins was conscious for a few minutes, but by the time the ambulance arrived and they were speeding to the hospital he had lost it completely.

Once Atkins reached New York Weill-Cornell Medical Center several blocks away, he was rushed by surgeons into the operating room and emergency surgery was performed to remove a blood clot from his brain. Afterward, doctors admitted the prognosis was not good. Atkins remained in a coma.

"Half his head was gone, half his brain had to be taken off," said Veronica. "I mean, the cranium certainly was gone, it was a severe, severe, severe trauma to the head."

Once the news hit, patients and fans of the diet from around the world visited the center's Web site and jammed the phone lines for any news of the doctor's condition.

"We are hoping for a miracle, but the chances for a meaningful recovery are slim," Richard Rothstein, a spokesman for the Atkins Center, told the media on April 11, three days after the fall.

Administering fluids on a twenty-four-hour basis is standard procedure when a patient is in a coma, and they caused his body to swell up to the point that friends had trouble recognizing him. Veronica would later say that his hands looked like ham hocks.

Longtime friend Warren Levin visited Atkins in the hospital the Saturday after his fall. "I wanted to make sure that he was getting the kind of alternative care that he would have wanted to get. And it was extraordinary. The cooperation we got from the top of Cornell on down to do whatever Mrs. Atkins wanted was wonderful."

The fact that Atkins received the best treatment available, both traditional and alternative—a concept he had long practiced at the center—was of little consolation. Ultimately, one outcome was inevitable.

Atkins was hooked up to life support for a few more days, as Veronica, coworkers, and friends took turns saying good-bye.

One by one, the life-support machines were turned off. He died, and his body was cremated the next day.

* * *

A memorial service for Dr. Robert Atkins was held in the Kaufman Concert Hall of the 92nd Street Y in Manhattan on May 9, 2003. Photographs of Atkins, taken at different times in his life, greeted guests as they entered.

The theme of the service was "To Dream the Impossible Dream," and it's estimated that close to a thousand people attended the service. The hall was filled with flowers, on stage and off.

The service was also filled with music, performed by concert pianist Clive Lithgoe, and Alison Buchanan, an opera singer, sang "The Impossible Dream."

Video clips of Atkins were interspersed with remembrances offered by friends and patients. Paul Wolff also spoke.

At the time of Robert Atkins's death, the Atkins Center boasted a roster of four thousand patients who visited the office for examinations and updates at least twice yearly.

Since the practice was under the umbrella of Atkins Nutritionals, headed up by Paul Wolff and Scott Kabak, it was up to them and Veronica to decide what to do with the practice. New York state law dictates that a medical practice must be closed temporarily following the death of the principal, but the decision to sell the practice or close it permanently rests with the executor and the company.

Keith Berkowitz, who had been working at the center briefly, quickly let it be known that he wanted to buy the practice. He claimed he and Atkins had discussed the possibility of him becoming the heir apparent, but others didn't believe him. As one former colleague scoffed at the account: "Atkins did that with everyone, just to feel them out."

Regardless of what Atkins's true intentions might have been, Veronica, Wolff, and Kabak began negotiating with Dr. Berkowitz. Part of the deal involved dropping the Atkins name, since it would inevitably lead to confusion in the minds of potential patients as well as longtime consumers.

The parties agreed to terms and a closing date of October 4, 2003, was set. Papers were drawn up, with attorneys on both sides reviewing the contracts. On October 2, however, the company made a public announcement that there would be no sale and the practice would be closing down for good on October 15.

Though Berkowitz was shocked by the announcement, he had no legal recourse available to fight the company's decision. Six months later, he said he still didn't know why they had pulled the rug out from underneath him at the last minute. Atkins Nutritionals didn't offer any explanation at the time, though company spokesman Richard Rothstein later said that the deal fell through because of money issues.

The official party line was that the center was shut down instead of sold because it was Robert Atkins's first love, and to continue without him just didn't make sense. However, continuing the food arm of the business did make sense since Atkins was never really that involved in it. No mention was made, of course, of his dismay at what his "hobby" had become, but skeptics believed that company executives probably heaved a big sigh of relief because they no longer had to placate Atkins by continuing with the center, then having to figure out the best way to make it seem like it wasn't losing as much money as it was.

A former center employee believes that even without the Atkins name, Berkowitz was not the best choice to carry the torch forward. In an article about the company since Atkins's death that ran in *Inc.*, a magazine for entrepreneurs, Berkowitz was described as "brash." Others felt that he didn't deserve the crown, having worked by Atkins's side for only a month.

"I think that Veronica got mad at Berkowitz, because after Atkins died, he was all over the newspapers saying he was Bob's personal this and personal that, and Veronica didn't care for that," said the former employee. "Keith thought he would be the one to take over the practice, and hints were dropped that it wasn't going to turn out that way. But Keith didn't really want to believe it, which is why the deal was called off."

In any case, patients were informed they should pick up their files, and they were given a list of other physicians they could see. Alphabetical, the first name on the list was Keith Berkowitz. Many of Dr. Atkins's patients did go over to Berkowitz's new practice, which he christened the "Center for Balanced Health," especially those who worked closely with him at the center, something he attributes to basic patient comfort level.

"There was a lot of confusion when the center was closed, but that soon began to clear," said Berkowitz. "I think patients tended to follow the doctor they knew best and who they were most comfortable with."

In any case, the closing of the center marked the end of one era. And the beginning of a fragmented, thoroughly confusing new one.

10.

THE BATTLE

FOR THE LOW-CARB CROWN

U sually, when a man dies, even if he is the most-hated guy around, there is no reason to kick him around anymore.

Even though Robert Atkins was dead, the monster he had created was very much alive and kicking. Suddenly, everyone wanted to get in bed with the beast. And those who didn't had no problem beating him down.

For decades, Dr. Atkins had the low-carb mantle all to himself. Even before his diet was proven to be scientifically sound, droves of competitors were trying to ride his coattails. They rushed into the marketplace with books to sell and practices to promote. Some succeeded, especially if they were among one of his longtime disciples.

These newcomers used to be clearly second-tier, but after Atkins died all bets were off and the race was on to become his replacement. It soon got nasty.

Manufacturers got a little crazy with the foods, too. It was almost as if since Atkins wasn't around anymore to defend himself and to assign blame where it counted, companies large and small decided to get in on the act, which resulted in some truly ridiculous claims about food. And some of the worst offenders were companies that were suffering the most due to the low-carb craze.

"Today there are fish oil supplements that the manufacturer says are low carb, which is like saying pretzels have no cholesterol," said Kurt Greenberg. "This is how absurd it gets. It just goes to show how gullible the public and food manufacturers can get."

"Because the bread and pasta industries are suffering economically," added Arline Brecher, "Atkins has become even more controversial today than when he was alive."

Since the aim of Atkins Nutritionals from the first day that Scott Kabak and Paul Wolff showed up for work was to distance Atkins the company from Atkins the man, his death obviously made their jobs a whole lot easier.

At the same time, there are those who feel that the company is clearly lacking since losing its most colorful spokesman. No one else was as heavily invested in low-carb as Atkins was.

"From a business point of view, I think Atkins Nutritionals suffers as a brand because there is nobody to identify with it," said Fred Pescatore. "The Atkins brand was always something that the public could connect with a real person, and unless they can overcome that, I think it's going to continue to be a real problem."

Even though Stuart Trager became the official physician spokesman for Atkins Nutritionals after the doctor's death, and even though his own personal low-carb transformation is credible, the fact that he originally had been an orthopedic surgeon and never actually worked with Atkins at the center makes him less than sufficient in the eyes of many.

Longtimers who were at the company before and after Atkins's death say that the corporate culture abruptly changed from one of fun and openness to one of stuffiness and a formal policy of toeing the party line. On the one hand, it isn't uncommon after a company's founder dies for employees to circle in a holding pattern while the future direction of the company is hashed out.

But this decision appeared to be final, apparently very much to do with the deal Atkins was discussing on the flight home from Florida just two days before he fell on the ice. At the time, employees knew a deal was in the offing sometime in the near future, but the top brass knew it was important to protect the corporate image, indeed, to make the Atkins Nutritionals corporate culture as bland as most other corporations, thereby making it more attractive to deep-pocketed investors.

Center employees cooperated fully, mostly because of the stock options they would receive as part of their benefits package. They didn't want to do anything to rock the boat. Or, more likely, word came down from on high to keep their mouths shut and clear everything through them.

Savvy investors know that when a majority interest is secured in a fast-growing company, it's only a matter of a year or two before that company goes public in order to handsomely pay off the original investors. News reports differed as to whether this would happen to Atkins. Some company sources claimed the company definitely would be going public within a year after the initial infusion of cash, while later reports pushed the IPO further into the future.

In October 2003, that future was permanently altered when the pending deal became reality. Parthenon Capital, a private investment firm, teamed up with Goldman Sachs Capital Partners to buy a majority interest in Atkins Nutritionals. The purpose of the sale primarily was to free up money for the foundation so that funding of outside studies could proceed and to fund Atkins Nutritionals' research and development, to keep on track with plans to introduce at least a hundred new low-carb foods each year.

Once the company was out from under its founder, it truly was full speed ahead. Not only was a new line of products being developed for the company, the Atkins name was also licensed out to Fortune 500 companies that could easily, quickly, and effectively blanket the country, which would also help to bolster the value of any future stock offering.

However, several food industry executives have cautioned Atkins Nutritionals publicly to be extremely careful handling the future of the company, despite the screaming demand for low-carb products. "The Atkins name confers trust," Richard Sneed, the CEO of the parent company of T.G.I. Friday's restaurant chain, told *BusinessWeek* in late 2003.

While diluting the value of the Atkins name by making it ubiquitous could quickly make trust disappear, other physicians also disagreed with the trail that Atkins Nutritionals was currently blazing.

"I regret that the products that the company is selling now don't emphasize the organic aspect of the food, which is what he taught all along," said Warren Levin. "I don't know at what point Atkins would have put his foot down, but I don't think that the current products are in keeping with his writings about the importance of avoiding processed foods. And that's ultimately going to tarnish the work that he did."

The one truly altruistic aspect to the sale of the company is that the Atkins Foundation suddenly found itself with much more money than it knew what to do with. In late 2004, the assets of the foundation stood at forty million dollars. Veronica Atkins had resigned earlier from the board of Atkins Nutritionals in order to make the foundation her sole focus. And because the amount of money in the foundation coffers was so significant, she decided to contract out its management to the National Philanthropic Trust.

A direct result of the increased funding was that the studies could be much broader in scope. Instead of just focusing on the diet and its effects, now studies focused on how a low-carb diet might affect a particular illness or disease.

"We've recently funded a study on epilepsy and seizures in both children and adults and another on cognitive functioning in the elderly," said Abby Bloch. Other studies explored how a low-carb diet could ease acid reflux disease, or the occurrence of obesity and type II diabetes in children.

Dr. Bloch was frustrated that despite conducting and closely monitoring studies according to strict scientific protocols, many in the professional community still believe that the primary focus of the foundation is to bolster Atkins Nutritionals sales, even though the two are totally separate entities.

"Mrs. Atkins walked away from anything that involved the company specifically so there would be no link to the foundation," said Dr. Bloch, who then told of the intense scrutiny she underwent by her colleagues at a conference of the American Dietetic Association. She sat on a panel addressing the low-carb phenomenon with two other speakers, yet the audience singled her out with negative questions and criticism just because she represented the Atkins Foundation.

Bloch tried to explain the differences between Atkins the company and Atkins the foundation, but to no avail. "It was very frustrating," she said. "They couldn't get beyond the fact that it was Atkins, and refused to give me the benefit of the doubt that I was furthering research and not selling bars or shakes. I don't know what else I can do. I'm trying to encourage researchers to talk to their colleagues and explain that the foundation is a research-driven organization and we're not selling bars and shakes and books, but it's been a very hard sell."

Indeed, this has also been the case with other venues as well, even in the upper echelons of New York City government. When Mayor Michael Bloomberg was eating a dinner of spaghetti and meatballs with a group of New York City firefighters in January 2004, one of the firefighters commented that the late Dr. Atkins wouldn't approve of the pasta.

Bloomberg, probably in an effort to feel like he was one of the guys during the photo op, but also assuming that the numerous television and video cameras were turned off during the meal, said that he thought the real reason for the doctor's death was covered up, that the explanation offered to the public, that Atkins slipped on the sidewalk, was, in his words, "bullshit."

"I don't believe that bullshit that he dropped dead after slipping on the sidewalk," said the mayor. "Yeah, right. The guy was fat. Big guy, but heavy."

Bloomberg then added that, in his opinion, the food that was served during a Republican fund-raiser he had attended at the Atkinses' lush estate in the Hamptons a couple of years earlier was inedible, and that he had to spit it into a napkin.

Mayor Bloomberg's words were broadcast on NY1 News that evening, and the only questions the media had for him at a press conference the next day concerned those remarks.

Veronica was livid. She appeared on *Good Morning America* on Friday that week to say that the mayor's comments were very hurtful and that she was very angry. She then demanded an apology. He refused. Finally, sometime the following week, Bloomberg decided to bury the hatchet and through his press secretary—not directly— he invited Mrs. Atkins to a steak dinner, no potatoes, his treat.

Though she initially agreed to take the mayor up on his offer, Veronica later said that something had come up and she had to cancel the dinner. It's not known whether they ever actually did meet up, but Bloomberg did later say, "I think that was an event that, uh, we should move on from here."

A few weeks later, the media flurry around Atkins resumed, and it showed just how determined his opponents were in still going after him even though he had been dead for almost a year. The openly anti-Atkins group Physicians for Responsible Medicine secured a copy of his death certificate and the confidential report from the city medical examiner and released it to the *Wall Street Journal.* It seemed that every media outlet in the country printed or aired the story.

Late in 2003, a Dr. Richard Fleming, of the Fleming Heart and Health Institute, sent a request for a copy of Robert Atkins's death certificate and medical report to the New York City Medical Examiner's office. Normally, the law prohibits medical examiners from releasing these records to no one but the immediate family, the individual's physician, or a state or federal agency that has a bona fide reason for reviewing the materials.

An assistant with the medical examiner's office, perhaps not familiar with the law, sent a copy to Fleming by mistake, which set off what would turn into a huge media circus in early February 2004. When Fleming received the report, he passed it on to the Physicians Committee for Responsible Medicine, a pro-vegetarian, anti-Atkins organization. After they reviewed the report, they faxed a copy to the *Wall Street Journal,* and then sat back to watch the sparks fly.

It caused an immediate uproar. News media from all over the world converged on the Atkins camp to get their side of the story.

"Wow," said Stuart Trager. "I never saw anything like it. I couldn't believe how interested the media was in the story."

Veronica was incensed. "[They are] unscrupulous individuals who continue to twist and pervert the truth." She also compared the group to the Taliban. "They're the vegetarian Taliban. I mean, I shouldn't insult vegetarians, but they are like the Taliban, these people. They're nasty."

The other side also presented its view. "I'm concerned about the Atkins machine trying to play the card that Atkins was healthy and thin into old age," said Dr. Neal Barnard, president of the Physicians Committee and a longtime rabid enemy of Atkins. He regarded the Atkins diet as an imminent threat to public health.

These incidents surely proved that those who believed the controversy over a low-carb diet ended when Dr. Atkins died were wrong. Fred Pescatore believes that the criticism and personal attacks continued because of Atkins's personality, and also because he was no longer around to defend himself or his diet.

"He was a very charismatic guy, and there are people with their own agendas to promote who are not willing to concede that after all of these years that he may have been right," said Dr. Pescatore. He also blames the food conglomerates and the fast food industry. "The Atkins way of life necessarily means a drastic change in the way food is delivered to our tables must take place, and that isn't going to happen overnight. In the meantime, they're kicking and screaming and sometimes resorting to pretty low tactics."

Indeed, just as certain food industries had benefited from the low-fat craze of the 1980s and '90s, numerous sectors were thrilled with the country's new obsession with everything low-carb. John B. Sanfilippo & Son is a Chicago company that packages nuts to supermarkets. Due to Atkins's pronouncement that nuts are important to a low-carb diet, the price of shares in Sanfilippo increased by over five hundred percent in 2003 alone.

On the flip side, shareholders in pasta companies were quick to dump their stocks once the sheer popularity of low-carb became apparent. In early 2004, shares in Monterey Pasta were down sixteen percent from a year earlier, and it doesn't take much of a look at a stock analyst's report on the company to figure out why.

"There's not much growth in the food industry," Prudential Securities stock analyst John M. McMillin told *BusinessWeek* in December 2003, "and Atkins is getting most of it."

Low-carb foods—those produced by Atkins Nutritionals as well as everything from small companies to huge conglomerates—were going gangbusters. According to Marketing Intelligence Service, a national market research firm, 1,865 new products described as being low in carbohydrates were introduced in the first six months of 2004 alone, 250 new low-carb products over the previous year. Of course, these new products don't include foods already on the market that merely have been relabeled "low-carb" by their manufacturers, everything from vegetable oil to fresh deli roast beef. Referring to these foods as low-carb was redundant, since they never contained carbohydrates in any measurable amounts.

A sign of where things were headed quietly surfaced in Boca Raton, Florida, back in 1997 when the first low-carb retail store in the country opened for business. Seven years later, an estimated three hundred low-carb stores had opened all across the country. In California, a chain called Castus Low Carb Superstores christened its first retail outlet in January 2004, with franchising plans that encircle the globe.

To help store owners and others learn about the trend from a business point of view, *LowCarbiz* publisher Dean Rotbart held the first of what he hopes will be many annual industry trade shows in January 2004, known as the "Low-Carb Business Summit."

Even sushi restaurants have jumped on the low-carb bandwagon. At Ace Wasabi's Rock 'n' Roll restaurant in San Francisco, chefs started to tinker with the standard fish-and-rice fare when patrons were leaving most of the rice behind uneaten on their black lacquered plates. Kiyoshi Hayakawa, owner and executive chef, developed low-carb versions of sushi where vegetables would stand in for the rice and seaweed but still resemble a traditional hand roll. He christened one of his creations "Daikori Maki," where raw tuna was encircled by a sliver of daikon radish. To get his point across further, he listed the amount of carbohydrate grams in each piece of sushi on the menu next to the price.

Perhaps the real sign that low-carb has permeated every corner of American life is that you can now purchase low-carb pet food. And QVC, the cable shopping network, offers a "Low-Carb Hour" several times each week.

The explosion in popularity of low-carb foods hasn't just been confined to the United States, of course. In December 2003, just as the prime dieting month of January loomed on the horizon, the legacy of Dr. Atkins became clear in Great Britain as news hit the newspapers of the imminent distribution of Atkins Nutritionals products on food shelves throughout the U.K. Customers who made up the estimated two million Brits who were reported to be following the diet at that time immediately began reserving cases of Atkins milkshakes, energy bars, and the bake mix, even though products weren't even going to reach retail stockrooms until mid-January. In fact, one of the major chains carrying the products had requested that the press hold off on publicizing the news until early in the new year, but, once word leaked out, it was anything goes and store managers braced themselves for the inevitable hordes.

Even though Robert Atkins was no longer alive, his representatives were forced to continue the job of toning down his more iconically outrageous statements as if he still were. At the same time, Atkins Nutritionals was accused of toning down the steak-and-eggs approach that Atkins had emphasized for years.

"Atkins has never been a red meat, all-you-can-eat diet," Stuart Trager told *Newsday* in January 2004. "It's about a nutritional approach that controls carbohydrates through a variety of food choices. We're not changing our message at all."

Maybe not, but it was quite apparent that even if he were still alive to do that interview, Atkins would not have put it that way. It is not surprising that the company was being accused of tinkering with its message.

Even as it had become clear that anyone promoting a low-carb diet would have to be defensive a good deal of the time, contenders were lining up to replace Atkins as spokesperson. As expected, many of his colleagues and supporters found this troubling.

"He stood by himself for so long, and very few others were

willing to jump into the water and stand there with him," said Stuart Trager. "What we're seeing now is that there are a lot of copycats who want to take credit for getting involved, but I think what we really should be doing is paying tribute to him for the battle he fought."

Jonny Bowden, M.A., author of *Living the Low Carb Life*, disagrees. "I think what they're all doing is raising the Atkins umbrella higher and higher. With the success of each copycat who has tried to either reformat the Atkins nutritional approach or misrepresent it so they can claim a portion of it as their own, they're just paying tribute to his approach. At the same time, this is no longer about an individual—any individual—but about the science, the theory, and the approach."

In *Living the Low Carb Life*, Bowden analyzed fourteen of the most popular low-carb diets, presenting their pros and cons, and then he described the type of person who would tend to do best on each one. "I tried to look at the diets that made the most sense, those that were user-friendly, easiest to follow, and so on, to give people a sense of which might be the best match," he said. Bowden automatically crossed some off his list, for a variety of reasons.

"I didn't include *The Perricone Prescription* in the book, because I felt it was wasn't primarily known as a diet book, but a skin book," he explained.

While dermatologist Nicholas Perricone admitted that his approach differs from the standard Atkins diet, he added that they are inherently cut from the same cloth. He, too, refers to refined sugar and white flour as "the white devil," and he stresses that salmon, not huge chunks of strip steak, is best for a low-carb diet. And he also called Atkins his hero. What's particularly interesting about that statement is that in December 2002 Atkins said he had never heard of Dr. Perricone, suggesting perhaps Atkins was still so focused on getting the word out that he had no energy or desire to learn about the eager new low-carb proponents coming up the backstretch.

Returning to the contenders, Jonny Bowden said he was not a big fan of the *Carbohydrate Addicts Diet*. "I gave it three stars for effort, but I found that the whole idea of eating two low-carb meals a day and then having anything you want for the third meal as long as it lasts less than an hour was filled with holes. It's like telling an alcoholic to be sober twenty-three hours a day, but for one hour a day you can go to town."

Many people believe that the runaway success of *The South Beach Diet* in early 2004 meant that its author, Arthur Agatston, M.D., would be Atkins's surefire successor. To be sure, Bowden awarded the diet five stars in his book. "While Atkins is much stronger on nutrition and vitamins, on the other hand, South Beach is very user-friendly," he said. "More importantly, Agatston was able to un-antagonize traditional physicians who automatically objected to it because it's similar to Atkins. After all, there's still a great deal of prejudice against Atkins in the conventional medical community, and South Beach introduced a low-carb diet in a way that was very breezy."

"The South Beach diet is a wonderful tribute to the Atkins approach because what it does is it talks about Atkins for life," said Stuart Trager. "South Beach absolutely describes the fourth phase of Atkins . . . the maintenance phase."

But with the success of *The South Beach Diet*, Veronica was clearly miffed. "Dr. Agatston didn't credit Bobby anywhere in the book."

Of course, the question begs to be asked: If Atkins were still alive, would *The South Beach Diet* be as popular as it turned out to be?

While there is no clear-cut answer to that question, in the end perhaps it isn't some diet offering a slight variation on the Atkins diet that eventually will be crowned the winner of the low-carb wars. It could be someone who not only stood by Atkins during his lean years but also is still actively involved in the low-carb industry but without a book to sell.

Fran Gare runs The Sweet Life, a small company that produces low-carb bake mixes and desserts. Her roots go way back; she first became a patient of Dr. Atkins in 1968, then worked for his practice, ultimately becoming the director of the Atkins Center and serving as his coauthor on his books. She refers to herself as "the mother of low-carb baking," and says that the Johnny-come-latelys starting up businesses only after the trend began to catch on in early 2000 are nothing but charlatans.

But, in the end, those duking it out to sell the most books or appear on the most talk shows don't really matter that much. After all, Robert Atkins didn't want to be remembered as just a diet doctor— "I never wanted to be known as a diet doc," he once said. He wanted to be respected as a doctor of complementary medicine.

Warren Levin remembers having a lengthy conversation some twenty years ago at a Florida spa with a man he describes as a "titan of industry." Levin was describing the complementary medical techniques he was utilizing in his practice and how his patients were benefiting, and the man, who happened to be on the board of governors at Cornell Medical School, was intrigued. He said he was going to ask someone at the college to invite Levin to give a lecture to the students.

A few days after returning home, Levin received a note from a representative of the college that said, in effect, Sorry, but I can't have you lecture to my students, I think you would charm them away from their scientific approach.

Dr. Levin was used to such rejection two decades ago. Recently, he was especially heartened at the way that Cornell integrated alternative therapies into the orthodox treatment Atkins received when he was in a coma.

"We've come a long way," said Levin. "And I think Bob Atkins was one of the major forces that has ended up creating departments of alternative and complementary medicine in many medical schools and hospitals across the country, so it is a great legacy."

Fred Pescatore agreed. "I think he would like to be remembered as one of the forefathers of alternative medicine," he said. Though it sometimes seemed as though Atkins resented the attention that was paid to the diet and not to his complementary medical focus, Pescatore sees it differently.

"I don't think he resented it," he said. "After all, the diet gave him a platform that he could then use to talk about vitamins and complementary medicine. Without that attention, he wouldn't have had the same stage."

Though Robert Atkins rarely delved conversationally into spirituality, he did view his life's work as a calling.

"It's kind of a spiritual thing," he said. "I think I was given the assignment to make an impact on health care in the world. I do think it's a God-given assignment."

"I want him to be remembered for his courage," says Veronica Atkins. "He was fighting no matter how much abuse they heaped on him."

Notes

Research for the book came from a variety of sources: personal interviews, articles, transcripts, and Dr. Atkins's own books. All quotes are taken from there sources except for those cited below.

PROLOGUE

"as long as you don't swallow it": *The Super-Doctors*, p. 176.

1. HAIL TO THE LOW-CARB KING

"the kind of hunger I put up with": *Brandweek*, Oct. 20, 2003.
"his greatest fear, to be hungry": *Larry King Show*, Feb. 16, 2004.
"wore argyle socks, I would wear [them]": *Biography Magazine*, 2001.
"athletes rather than brains": *Dayton Daily News*, Feb. 20, 2003.
"I like gigantic towns": Ibid.

2. THE THIRTY-POUND BREAKTHROUGH

"that was a success": *Biography Magazine*, 2001.
"the more I ate, the more I lost": Ibid.

3. HAPPINESS IS A PURPLE STICK

"the privilege of going off it": *The Super-Doctors*, p. 189.
"keep the pears small": Ibid.
"and finally said okay": Ibid., p. 188.
"and say, 'Are you eating?' ": *Dayton Daily News*, Feb. 20, 2003.
"to reach the medical profession": *The Super-Doctors*, p. 184.

4. THE BRICKBATS FLY

"make any money on it": *The Super-Doctors*, p. 183.
"but on diets which were dissimilar": *New York Times*, March 10, 1973.
"it wasn't interest in the patients": *Let's Live*, Feb. 2001.
"would come to the fore": *The Super-Doctors*, p. 177.
"something to eat while we're being served": Ibid., p. 179.
"well-adjusted workaholic": *People*, Aug. 26, 1985.
"newly-acquired Rolls-Royce Silver Shadow II": Ibid.
"not . . . after the patient has died": *Challenging Orthodoxy*, p. 13.
"to his mother and father": *The Super-Doctors*, p. 192.
"visiting showrooms to get it just right": *New York Times*, March 5, 1978.

"become the overriding factor in my personality": *The Super-Doctors*, p. 179.

5. THE TWILIGHT ZONE

"And that's what we live by": *Challenging Orthodoxy*, p. 17.

"whatever he's got in there works": Ibid.

"I don't know how to make a profit": *Business 2.0*, Apr. 2003.

"and tend to be forgiving": *New York Times*, Nov. 27, 1996.

"He always goes for the shock value": *Business 2.0*, Apr. 2003.

"What is medicine, what is science, what is healing?": *Challenging Orthodoxy*, p. 18.

"the cure of an incurable illness": Ibid., p. 19.

"war against the establishment": Ibid., p. 20.

6. A PACT WITH THE DEVIL

"the problems health care has inherited": *New York Times*, Nov. 27, 1996.

7. THE SWEET SPOT

"second agenda to make a person look bad": *New York Times*, Nov. 27, 1996.

"We have transcended fad.": *Business 2.0*, Apr. 2003.

"take a concept and make it a brand": *Newsday*, 2003.

"like Kleenex is to facial tissue": *New York Times*, Jan. 4, 2004.

"selective citation to prove anything they want": *Total Health*, Nov./Dec. 2001.

"referred to his house as "so late-seventies": *New York Magazine*, March 15, 2004.

"actually very low in fat": *New York Magazine*, Dec. 16, 2002.

"pasta is a junk food": *Publishers Weekly*, Feb. 3, 2003.

"a great deal of satisfaction": *The Phil Donahue Show*, Jan. 29, 2003.

8. The Planets Align: July 7, 2002

"Stop eating carbohydrates!": *Washington Post*, Apr. 18, 2003.

"dream a little bigger" : *Business 2.0*, Apr. 2003.

"because so many people are on Atkins": *New York Magazine*, Dec. 16, 2002.

"the greatest story ever": Ibid.

"I'm on the verge of succeeding": *Business 2.0*, Apr. 2003.

9. The Last Days

"It was frustrating to all of us": *New York Magazine*, March 15, 2004.

"something that heartened him immensely": *Brandweek*, Oct. 20, 2003.

"severe, severe, severe trauma to the head": *Larry King Show*, Feb. 16, 2004.

10. THE BATTLE FOR THE LOW-CARB CROWN

"we should move on from here": *New York Times*, Feb. 11, 2004.

"twist and pervert the truth": Ibid.

"they are like the Taliban, these people. They're nasty": *Dateline NBC*, Feb. 20, 2004.

"an imminent threat to public health": *New York Times,* Feb. 11, 2004.

"the mother of low-carb baking": *Fortune*, Jan. 12, 2004.

"I never wanted to be known as a diet doc": *Washington Post*, Apr. 18, 2003.

"a God-given assignment": *Let's Live*, Feb. 2001.

"how much abuse they heaped on him": *People*, May 5, 2003.

Timeline of Dr. Atkins's Life

1930 Born October 17 in Columbus, Ohio.

1951 Graduated from the University of Michigan.

1955 Received medical degree from Cornell University Medical School.

1960 Opened private practice in New York City.

1963 Discovered low-carbohydrate diet and lost twenty-eight pounds in six weeks.

1972 *Dr. Atkins' Diet Revolution*, his first book, is published.

1977 *Dr. Atkins' Super Energy Diet* published.

1981 *Dr. Atkins' Nutrition Breakthrough* published.

1984 Changed focus of practice to alternative medicine with opening of the Atkins Center for Complementary Medicine.

1988 Married Veronica Luckey.

1988 *Dr. Atkins' Health Revolution* published.

1992 *Dr. Atkins' New Diet Revolution* published.

1997 *Dr. Atkins' Quick and Easy New Diet Revolution Cookbook* is published with wife Veronica as coauthor.

1998 Complementary Formulations is renamed Atkins Nutritionals, Inc.

1998 *Dr. Atkins' Vita-Nutrient Solution: Nature's Answer to Drugs* published.

1999 Introduces a new edition of *Dr. Atkins' New Diet Revolution*.

1999 The Dr. Robert C. Atkins Foundation is launched.

2000 *Dr. Atkins' Age-Defying Diet Revolution* published.

2003 *Atkins for Life* published.

2003 Robert Atkins dies on April 17, 2003.

Dr. Atkins's Published Titles

Dr. Atkins' Diet Revolution

Dr. Atkins' Super Energy Diet

Dr. Atkins' Nutrition Breakthrough

Dr. Atkins' Health Revolution

Dr. Atkins' New Diet Revolution

Dr. Atkins' Quick and Easy New Diet Revolution Cookbook

Dr. Atkins' Vita-Nutrient Solution

Dr. Atkins' Age-Defying Diet Revolution

Atkins for Life

Atkins Diabetes Revolution (published posthumously)

Bibliography

Agatston, Arthur, M.D. *The South Beach Diet: The Delicious, Doctor-Designed, Foolproof Plan for Fast and Healthy Weight Loss.* Emmaus, Pa.: Rodale Press, 2003.

Atkins, Robert C., M.D. *Dr. Atkins' Diet Revolution.* New York: David McKay, 1972

———. *Dr. Atkins' Nutrition Breakthrough: How to Treat Your Medical Condition Without Drugs.* New York: William Morrow, 1981.

———. *Dr. Atkins' Health Revolution: How Complementary Medicine Can Extend Your Life.* New York: Bantam, 1990.

———. *Dr. Atkins' Vita-Nutrient Solution: Nature's Answer to Drugs.* New York: Simon & Schuster, 1999.

———. *Dr. Atkins' New Diet Revolution.* New York: Quill, 2002.

———. *Atkins for Life: The Complete Controlled Carb Program for Permanent Weight Loss and Good Health.* New York: St. Martin's Press, 2003.

———. *Atkins Diabetes Revolution: The Groundbreaking Approach to Preventing and Controlling Type 2 Diabetes.* New York: William Morrow, 2004.

Bibliography

Atkins, Robert C., M.D., and Fran Gare. *Dr. Atkins' Super Energy Diet*. New York: Crown, 1977.

Atkins, Robert C., M.D., and Veronica Atkins. *Dr. Atkins' Quick and Easy New Diet Revolution Cookbook*. New York: Fireside, 1997.

Atkins, Robert C., M.D., and Sheila Buff. *Dr. Atkins' Age-Defying Diet Revolution: A Powerful New Dietary Defense Against Aging*. New York: St. Martin's Press, 2001.

Bowden, Jonny, M.A. *Living the Low Carb Life*. New York: Sterling, 2004.

Greenberg, Kurt. *Challenging Orthodoxy: America's Top Medical Preventives Speak Out!* New Canaan, Conn.: Keats Health Book, 1991.

Heller, Richard F., M.D., and Rachael F. Heller, M.D. *The Carbohydrate Addict's Diet: The Lifelong Solution to Yo-Yo Dieting*. New York: Dutton, 1991.

Perricone, Nicholas. *The Perricone Prescription*. New York: HarperResource, 2002.

Pescatore, Fred, M.D. *Feed Your Kids Well: How to Help Your Child Lose Weight and Get Healthy*. New York: John Wiley & Sons, 1999.

———.*The Hamptons Diet: Lose Weight Quickly and Safely with the Doctor's Delicious Meal Plans*. New York: John Wiley & Sons, 2004.

Raphael, Marc Lee. *Jews and Judaism in a Midwestern Community: Columbus, Ohio, 1840–1975*. Columbus: Ohio Historical Society, 1979.

Rapoport, Roger. *The Super-Doctors*. Chicago: Playboy Press, 1975.

Acknowledgments

ost books have a raft of behind-the-scenes people who all had a hand in bringing the final product to fruition, but I think with a biography, by its very definition, the number of folks just seems to be exponentially more.

Ancestry.com provided a treasure trove of search possibilities to an American history nut like me. I could have spent weeks drilling down deep in its census records, newspaper archives, and immigration rosters, but, unfortunately, I had a book to write.

Marc Lee Raphael, author of *Jews and Judaism in a Midwestern Community: Columbus, Ohio, 1840–1975*, provided a marvelous context of Jewish life in the city when Atkins was a child, as well as the experiences of his parents, grandparents, and great-grandparents. Extra thanks go to Raphael for including a photo of a steerage ticket that had Coleman Tokerman's name scrawled on it. This helped me connect the man and his family to Dr. Atkins, and therefore trace the main source of Atkins's tremendous drive.

Editor Anna Cowles at Chamberlain Bros. deserves heaps of

praise for deciding to take this book under her wing when the imprint was still wet behind the ears.

Paula Hancock did a superb job of making sense of the taped interviews and provided me with clean transcripts that made writing this book much easier.

Genealogist Carolyn J. Burns dug through countless dusty stacks and documents in Dayton and Columbus to meticulously trace the all-important lineage of Atkins's predecessors as well as obscurities like the street addresses of bars and cigar shops in 1942.

Scott Mendel must have the lowest blood pressure of any agent in the world, because he listened to my numerous rants and raves and lurid descriptions of various personal crises without once getting flustered. Many thanks for shepherding the book through the convoluted maze that is publishing.

Thanks to Ronald Arky, M.D., Keith Berkowitz, M.D., Abby Bloch, M.D., Jonny Bowden, M.A., C.N.S., Arline Brecher, Stuart Fischer, M.D., Fran Gare, Kurt Greenberg, Betty Kamen, Judith Klopp, Warren Levin, M.D., Shirley Linde, Len Lipson, Fred Pescatore, M.D., Robert Rafner, Roger Rapoport, Bernard Raxlen, M.D., Maryann Raxlen, Barbara Stinson, Gary Taubes, Stuart Trager, M.D., Loretta Weber, Eric Westman, M.D., and many others for telling me what they remembered about the time they spent with Dr. Atkins.

Final kudos go to Gregg Ramsay for putting up with the cats, cars, coffee, chianti, and even the coffins, and for thinking it's perfectly fine whenever I catch a particularly intriguing scent and go flying off on yet another tangent . . . that is, until the next one comes along.